The Muslim Mind Presents
Instant Insights
by Dr T K Harris

Thanks to my dearest friend, Mufti Ismail Menk, without whose inspiration and allegiance through my own tough times, I could not have written this book.

"Truly an awesome achievement. Harris has combined modern mental health with Islamic principles in such an elegant way... as to make the connection totally natural."
- Safia Parker

"The book I wish I had when I was a younger adult. Insight follows insight with every word. I will give it to my children, and urge every reader to do the same."
-Shaheen Malik

"True to its title, it really is immediately helpful. Read it and never fear your emotions or hardships again".
-David Salam-Carmine

"Give this gift to yourself. It will ease your mind in so many ways, and change your life for the better. Alhamdulillah."
- Nouman Hafeez

First Edition Published January 2020.

Oxford, UK.

Muslim Mind
www.muslim-mind.webnode.com

Instant Insights

The Muslim Mind Guide
for Success and Contentment
in testing times

For H, Y and L.
Your love, support and patience are enough to fill the Universe.
I thank Allah that you have been alive and well through our tough times.
I pray that He helps us through all times ahead.

For Dad, Mum, A, N, S & S.

Contents

The basic model in this book.

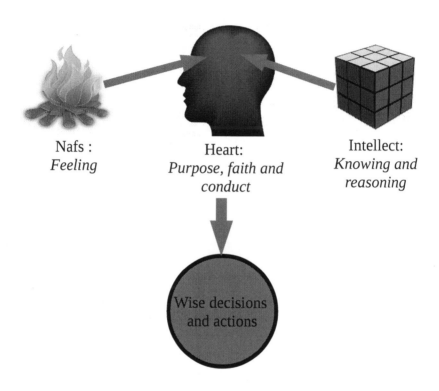

Nafs :
Feeling

Heart:
*Purpose, faith and
conduct*

Intellect:
*Knowing and
reasoning*

Wise decisions
and actions

Preface

The Arabic word for 'human being' is *Insaan*. The word actually comes from the verb *nasiya* meaning 'forget'. There is deep Godly wisdom in this: surely it is our basic nature as human beings to forget, and make mistakes. Linguists also tell us that Insaan comes from the word *uns* which means *to tame, to become familiar with.*

In the Quran, *Insaan* refers to the sum total of characteristics and conduct of man in the real world. We are designed exactly in the way Allah intended. Let us examine some of the things that the Quran says about the base instincts and nature of man:

"And man has been created weak (lacking firmness to control his vain desires and passions)."
Surah 4: Verse 28
"Indeed, man has been created impatient and anxious."
Surah 70: Verse 19
"Surely, man is very unjust and ungrateful."
Surah 14: Verse 34
"And man is ever miserly."
Surah 17: Verse 100
"And man, in most cases, is contentious and quarrelsome."
Surah 18: Verse 54
"Surely, he is very unjust and ignorant (lacking thought and deliberation)." Surah 33: Verse 72

These verses are not criticisms of man: they are simply statements of fact.

Alhamdulillah. We must praise Allah for his accurate portrayal of the state of Man. This is exactly how we are meant to be. From the very outset, we realise that we are created with our individual faults and quirks exactly as He intended for us. How could this be a blessing?

Being prone to mistakes is written into the very character that Allah has designed us to have. If He accepts us in this way, then we are to accept ourselves in this state. What should we look at in order to be the best we can be?

Well, we have also been given two other crucial things: *free will,* and *instructions*. Free will is the ability to decide how we want to think about things, and how we wish to be in this world. Instructions come in the form of our religion, and from our inner, higher instincts: the things that we can all agree make for a good person. All sane human beings, religious or not, are capable of having have *higher qualities* such as morality, kindness and compassion. Islam gives us more detailed guidance: it makes clear the direction in which we should aim our thinking and behaviour.

And so our mission in life emerges. Our great privilege, in being the highest of all Allah's creations, is that we have the free will to earn Allah's favour and pleasure by overcoming challenges, and maximising the good we can do, through the mental capabilities he has given us. Along the way, He knows perfectly well that we will definitely mess up, make mistakes, but He is only too ready to help us along when we make mistakes or bad judgments.

We are forgiven the instant we ask for forgiveness and resolve to be wiser next time. We are commanded to simply do our best, to be as wise and attentive as we can be, in dealing with whatever circumstances and events life throws at us.

The point to make here is that we must be sympathetic to our reality. We cannot hope to become free of fault; in fact every fault and foible within us is part of our makeup, and our life's journey is to improve ourselves in our behaviour, conduct and our faith, knowing that we still have our tensions and deficiencies within us until our last breath.

It is not our aim to become perfect, or to expect that the world around us behaves in the way we would like. This is unrealistic, and moreover very unkind to our wellbeing: perfectionism and high expectations are a recipe for sadness and frustration. We earn Allah's pleasure, and we become content and happy, simply by making humble daily efforts to be as good as we can, taking the world as we find it.

We must not, for one moment, feel that this is somehow too great a task. Alhamdulillah, we have been given all we need by Allah: we simply need to apply it. If we pay attention to learn and apply this understanding to our lives, then we will surely become wise, content, and successful, in this world and in the hereafter. Ameen.

The book has a central model by which its various chapters are framed. The model is that there are three basic ingredients to the human mind, from lowest to highest: otherwise known as *Nafs*, *Intellect*, and *Heart* respectively.

The model is based on both religious and scientific roots. For the first, we have considered the descriptions of the human mind that are offered in the Quran, and the Hadith. Nafs, Heart and Intellect are repeatedly referred to, throughout Islamic teachings. Their nature and interactions have been the subject of many deep and beautiful thoughts and teachings by Islamic thinkers. This book draws on those teachings, concentrating on the aspects within the mind: how to understand and manage your mind to be as effective and mentally fit as you can be for the sake of your love of Allah.

Scientifically, there is plenty of good basis for this model too. Over many hundreds of years of research, both Islamic and secular academics and experts have together discovered many useful ways to describe the mind, and devised elegant and effective ways to help people to manage their minds in a way that helps them achieve contentment, peace, and success.

As a cautionary note, this book is not about trying to create a false or forced connection between Islamic concepts and scientific ones. **Science does not require faith, and faith does not require science.** Rather, we have shown that there are parallels which make Islamic and scientific views quite readily compatible, as far as we know them. In this effort, the book is using the best of scientific knowledge of good mental functioning and merging it with the Islamic framework of the same matter, to help the intelligent Muslim reader be more effective in achieving contentment and success in life. Alhamdulillah.

The very idea of Nafs, for example, has got numerous components and parallels that are described in scientific theories and discoveries about the emotional and instinctive functions of the brain. Nafs is the collection of emotions, instincts and drives that every human being is born with. In a biological sense, we can even describe how the functions of the Nafs are localised in different regions of the brain and body. The same can be said of Intellect (intelligence) and Heart (self-awareness and purpose).

Sufi thinking brings us some particularly insightful views on how to achieve inner peace. For example *muraqabah* (see Chapter 10) which Sufi teachers have practised for centuries, is the same as modern descriptions of *mindfulness*. Mindfulness has been extensively researched over the past 20 years in the best modern institutions from Harvard to Oxford, and it has been shown to have incredible benefits, even if practised in small amounts every day. It is proven scientifically and known religiously: practising mindfulness helps people to develop better self control, greater awareness of themselves, and to give greater attention to what really matters in the world around them.

Alhamdulillah, these discoveries and the methods of addressing issues such as happiness, goals and emotional difficulty, both inform and agree with Islamic knowledge on matters of the mind and human nature.

Scientific or religious experts may find this book lacking in the detail that they are used to. We have not set out to produce an encyclopedia of detail: rather, this book is a straightforward 'how to' guide on how to apply one's mind to everyday problems. As such, it is not meant to be authoritative to the last small detail of religion or science. Rather, we have tried to use the best overall guidance of scientific and religious knowledge, in our own humble endeavours and using simple techniques, to create unified and readily understood 'recipes for good mental health' in each chapter.

This book is a humble and best effort to be of use to our fellow Ummah to find happiness, contentment and success. There is no wish to contradict or stray from the teachings of those with greater learning: the reader is encouraged to read this work with an optimistic and open point of view, and to regularly pause, look upwards, and reflect on what they have just read, comparing it to their own knowledge and wisdom in the hope of gaining some helpful technique or insight to further their life in the path of being good people, of benefit to themselves and the ones they love, in the path of Allah. If this happens for even one person, we as authors and contributors would feel our mission accomplished.

We only need to be optimistic and humble, paying attention to ourselves and helping the people around us as we grow, to claim all of the benefits of this knowledge, by applying it steadily and humbly every day. The first step is already done: if you are reading this, you are already someone who is on this journey. Turning up, as they say, is half the victory.

Allah is the greatest authority, and we pray that he has given us enough guidance to produce a useful piece of work. We, the author and contributors, ask for forgiveness and tolerance if there are errors, omissions or departures in this work, and we hope for constructive criticism and guidance from the Ummah in refining it for future editions.

T K Harris
Feb 2020

What is life but a series of inspired small adventures?
Seek them, because they don't come every day.

Do not believe that those who seek to comfort you,
Have had a life of peace. They have endured difficulty.
They would not have found the right words otherwise.

Consider difficulties as blessings, just like the storm
Teaches the little plant to grow a strong stem.

Become your own king; know how to rule yourself!

If you don't set out to know yourself properly,
Allah is saddened. Neither you nor others will discover
The value he has placed in you.

Make the most of yourself,
For that is all that Allah has given to you.

Lend yourself to other people,
But give yourself fully to Allah.

Good things are achieved by she who believes that
Allah has not just created her as a meaningless act.

If you feel inadequate without gold and silver,
You will be just as inadequate with them.
True wealth is within you regardless of gold.

Chapter 1: Introduction

Bismillahir-Rahmaanir-Raheem.
In the name of Allah, the Beneficent, the Merciful.

Alhamdulillah! The aim of life is very clear to us, given as a gift by Allah. We are to live faithfully and considerately, to try to show good conduct, to adherence to Allah's guidance, and to aim to be of benefit to other people.

Accepting who we are

Unconditional acceptance of life and all it brings, is the basis of a successful and contented life. The very word Islam means *submission to Allah's way*. The word derives from the word *salm* which means *peace*. Submission means that we accept Allah's will, His instructions, and that He has given to us in this world. We are each born into our own individual circumstances, and we all have different events, advantages, setbacks and resources.

Islam requires that we each individually accept our different circumstances, and be thankful for them. Within the very word Islam, we therefore find the first kernel of truth:

Peace is found in accepting what Allah has given us.

Look around you. Most people are basically doing the best they can, in difficult circumstances. Accepting who we are, and setting out to find success in life, becomes easier when we understand what makes us tick. This is why we set out to write this book.

You need to start off from the truthful place: you need to accept yourself as an inherently good and worthy person, just as you are. No need to prove it, or justify it to anyone else. You are worthy just as you live and breathe. Look past your doubts, and get to this truth. Believe truly that you are, and always will be, a humble and *worthy* person, that you are *valuable with all your faults and strengths just as they are*. If you do this, you are showing a deeper understanding of the meaning of Islam: you gain a sense of self respect, and your actions become invested with a positive truth. This in turn helps you to become more optimistic and confident when you set out to achieve something.

There is no need to be frightened or scared into change: let nobody, including you, tell you that you are bad, worthless, or doomed, trying to put fear into your heart in order to get you to change. Fear might work in emergencies, but it does not work in the long term.

Your responsibility

You gain more control over your destiny when you accept that you are responsible for
- dealing with everything that happens to you
- everything that goes on in your head
- and everything you do.

1. INTRODUCTION

Your feelings, and your actions, and words are your responsibility. Even your unwanted feelings are your responsibility to deal with. If you cannot manage them, it is your responsibility to learn how, or to seek help from someone who can help. If you make an unwise decision, you are responsible for its consequences. If you took advice from someone and it turns out to be bad advice, you are still responsible for the action because you decided to go along with their advice.

Responsibility sounds like a burden, but it is really the opposite. When you take responsibility for yourself, you are gaining the power over your life. You can't control what life throws at you, nor what other people do and say or think about you, but you can and must take responsibility for as much of your life as is within your control. Equally, you must let go and feel completely free of the burden of controlling what other people say or do: that is their responsibility.

You do not control what other people say or feel. By showing good character, and emotional intelligence, you might indeed be of good influence on them, but still, you must accept the fact that whatever they do in the end is within their control.

You can influence what YOU say and feel. What someone else did right or wrong is not yours to change. They are part of the world that you can't take responsibility for. The only thing you can take responsibility for is what YOU do. This can only improve if you pay attention to investigate what you feel, say and do.

The benefits of being more accepting and more responsible

Suppose you have some money saved. You want to invest your money in the shares of a company, and you have a choice: company A or company B.

In company A, the employees only work properly when their bosses are mean to them, and where the bosses themselves don't think much of the future of the place. The company is working at a very quick pace which is difficult to keep up.

In company B, the employees feel valued, and work because they like working there. The employees get paid according to how well they do their job: their rewards are linked to their performance. The bosses take time to value the employees: progress may be slower, because people are taking more care to produce a quality product, but the place will keep growing steadily.

Which would you rather invest in if you were making a long term investment? A wise person would choose B.

Now think of yourself in the same way: do you believe in yourself? Are you kind to yourself, taking care of your mind and body, and are you content to work in a way that is slow and steady rather than urgent and panicked? And do you believe that you are better off taking control of your actions and character rather than leaving it to chance?

Just like a good company, you must consider what it takes to make **you** a worthy investment. This involves learning about your abilities, accepting and working with your limitations and faults as they are, becoming clear in your aims and conduct, and knowing what you can and can't change. Then, by trusting in Allah that everything in your life is exactly as He ordains it, whatever comes your way, you will do your best.

In embracing the knowledge you gain about yourself, and the reality of your world with all its problems and advantages, you begin to become **more closely matched** to your life. You will be able to use your mind, with all of its components: Nafs, Intellect and Heart, to live peacefully and contentedly, with wisdom and Deen written large in your heart.

Nothing is wasted, good or bad

No experience, no trauma, no good fortune, no memory, is wasted: you are indeed as perfect as the way Allah intended. It is our duty, not just an option, to say Alhamdulillah for all the things that have happened to us. We must try to understand our reality accurately, in clear and rational mind, and accept it once we know it.

Our emotions, our abilities, and our advantages and disadvantages as they are in our life, are all available for us to discover. It is only through self awareness, and accepting the lot that we are given, that we can set out to tackle the journey of life without becoming exhausted, without always feeling embattled.

It would be arrogant to believe that we have greater knowledge or insight over our lives than the Creator himself: the life we have, and the people we are, all come from His grace and will.

Be thankful and remember Allah at every turn

Whether you are young, old, sad, happy, rich or poor, remember to say Alhamdulillah to whatever you face.

When you encounter difficulty, saying Alhamdulillah reminds you that everything in your life is no accident, that everything that happens is well known to Allah. Difficulties are merely opportunities to show our character in a good light, and even apparent disasters are not as they seem. Time and time again, we see how adversity breeds opportunity and growth in people who are mindful, self aware, and humble.

When you encounter success, saying Alhamdulillah reminds you that even success is just an event, a transient thing, and not to become so convinced of your own ability that you become arrogant, lost in your own pride, attracting jealousy from others. You have the free will to act in any way you see fit; this book is about learning how best to manage yourself, in the world that you live in, to be as good as you can be, and to make humble efforts to achieve the things that you want to achieve.

The Muslim Mind

Allah has given us our brain: the main gift that separates us from the animals. How do we begin to take control of ourselves, to manage our minds and our behaviour, in a way that is sympathetic to how we are made?

We can't just simply do it with ignorant willpower and baseless hope. We can't just hope and pray to get better and then just expect that knowledge, wellbeing, success and happiness will just happen: we need to make efforts to learn, understand, and apply what we learn. This book is about that learning process.

If we don't act wisely, the most decisive actions in our life will be mindless, unconsidered, and we become purposeless, self-destructive, and lost. We would be nothing more than impulsive, selfish beings, existing purely to satisfy our immediate desires, causing untold destruction and cruelty, barely different from animals. This book is about understanding how to avoid being insightless and mindless.

There are many complex descriptions of how thinking and behaviour are generated in human beings. However for the purposes of understanding the mind, this simple model will be sufficient.

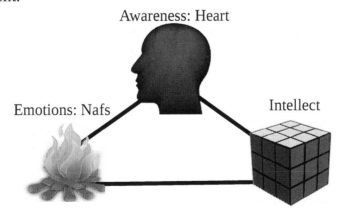

Awareness: Heart

Emotions: Nafs

Intellect

The mind is a magnificent creation of Allah. This model is a mere aid to understanding the mind, for the purposes of this guide. It will appear repeatedly throughout this book.

A human being's conduct and behaviour are the result of the interactions between the Nafs, the Intellect, and the Heart.

How the mind develops

In order of their development over time, the following picture describes the ideal situation of how the different parts of the mind develop

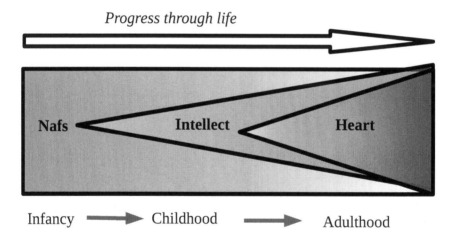

Progress through life

Nafs — Intellect — Heart

Infancy → Childhood → Adulthood

The Nafs, our emotions and instincts, is permanent, and omnipresent: it is there from birth, and stays with us until we die. Our life is spent trying to make the best of our emotions and instincts: trying to understand them, deal with them, and tame them from their excesses.

The Intellect, our intelligence, is dormant when we first are born, and then we begin to use it in the first few years of childhood. It is where we learn facts and rules, and where we learn how to solve problems, work with others, and become masterful at something. The child first develops Intellect through curiosity and play, exploring the world around it. As we get older, the Intellect rapidly develops, especially in things that it is naturally good at: we all have individual strengths and types of intelligence that we could develop and use to further ourselves. The more the Intellect is used, the better it gets.

The Heart, our **true awareness of ourselves**, is what we are measured on by Allah. We can choose to develop it, and if we do, the rewards are magnificent, both in material matters and matters of religion. The Heart is the seat of our wisdom, our purpose in life. It is also our inner eye, giving us our ability to police ourselves and be mindful of our actions and conduct. We are judged by Allah based on what is in our Heart. You should take the Heart to mean **your true, best self.**

The more you are aware of what is going on inside you and the world around you, the more you will become the best real version of you.

The journey of life

Alhamdulillah: Allah has set us all on a marvellous journey, full of possibilities and uncertainties, and opportunities for joy and sadness alike. This journey is called life: we must all do our best to develop ourselves, humbly and incrementally.

The key to great progress in life is this: **Tiny step by tiny step.**
I mean, really really small steps, being thankful all the way along
for each step taken.

We only live one minute at a time, so we cannot expect to
overcome great challenges or master great things any quicker
than one minute at a time. Slowly and steadily does it. We must
pause and reflect much more often than we currently do: it helps
us to refine our journey and stay true to our direction.

The most complete, peaceful person is described as having a
good heart. This person has attained a sense of self awareness,
and remembrance of Allah, and in so doing, is able to control
their Nafs and use their Intellect to greatest effect.

This is a lifelong effort, and very frequently, it feels like a battle.
We are constantly faced by temptations: we can become
persuaded to rely on just our emotions, acting impulsively and
rashly, causing chaos and instability for ourselves and those
around us. We could equally use our Intellect in an unwise way,
misusing our intelligence to accomplish hurtful or destructive
things for our own personal gain. Our Heart will be weak if we
do not consider our higher purpose, our missions in life, or the
way in which we choose to conduct ourselves. This book is about
how to understand these components of ourselves, and use them
to our best ability to be as good as we can be.

If it were easy, you wouldn't need books or guidance

It is unwise to think that becoming content and successful is easy: it requires constant, modest effort. We will learn, and fail to put our learning to use. We will make mistakes, some of which we will repeat time and time again. We will lose control of our wisdom when we are facing great elation or great sadness.

Alhamdulillah! This is all well known, predicted, and prescribed for us by Allah. Our life's journey requires us to do our best to manage ourselves towards wisdom, remembrance and practice of religion, and good conduct in achieving our aims in life. You get out what you put in.

Tips for being thankful to Allah in a deep and rich way.

- _Go for depth over breadth. Elaborating in detail about a particular thing for which you're grateful carries more benefits than a superficial list of many things._

- _Get personal. Focusing on people to whom you are grateful has more of an impact than focusing on things for which you are grateful._

- _Try subtraction, not just addition. One effective way of stimulating gratitude is to reflect on what your life would be like without certain blessings, rather than just tallying up all those good things._

- _Savour surprises. Remember events that were unexpected or surprising, as these tend to bring stronger levels of gratitude._

Remember things to be grateful for in every du'aa.
Being grateful to Allah invites Him
To bring you further favours.

If you don't accept responsibility for your actions,
You will grow tired of defending them.

Take control of your life.
Trusting in Allah does not mean
Leaving your camel untethered.

If you take ownership of your mind,
You can take ownership of anything else
Which Allah has promised you.

Accept yourself always,
Even when you feel unacceptable.
Allah accepts you always; are you wiser than He?

INSTANT INSIGHTS

Chapter 2: The Muslim Mind

We will now set out to understand how the mind is composed in more detail. In essence, for the purposes of simplified and easy understanding, this is the way in which wise decisions are made:

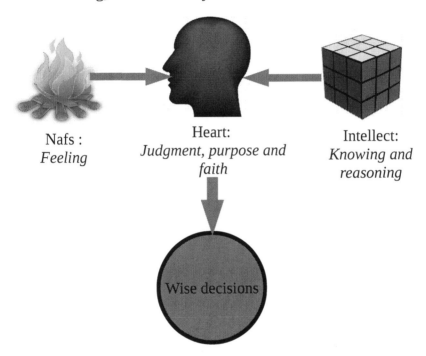

Nafs :
Feeling

Heart:
Judgment, purpose and faith

Intellect:
Knowing and reasoning

Wise decisions

As you can see, our decisions and actions are influenced by the three forces: our Nafs, our Heart, and our Intellect.

When we consider anything with the Heart, we look at both what the Nafs and the Intellect make of it. We add in our judgment, and look to our Deen and our purpose if we need to, before making a decision which is the best way forward, knowing what we know. We calmly accept the chance that we may be wrong.

By looking at both the emotional and the logical components, we can become aware of them fully, and we make a wise decision that is our best estimate of what to do, *feeling* right about it (Nafs) and *knowing* what's right about it (Intellect), and adding *judgment* and awareness of our faith (Heart). Sometimes the Nafs and Intellect will disagree: it is why we use the Heart to exercise a final judgment.

This process does not happen automatically. In fact, the natural scheme of things is more primitive: without guidance, we end up using the Nafs alone, or the Intellect alone.

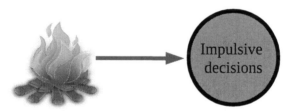

For most people, the Nafs is the most troublesome: it is rapid, mindless and tempting to act on the Nafs, leading us to make decisions based on nothing more than temptations or impressions, failing to consider the consequences, not considering morality, or missing the real facts. This might help to get us out of the occasional life-threatening situation, but in most cases it is a blunt and troublesome way to live.

The Nafs: our emotions, instincts and basic drives

The full name of the Nafs- the seat of our basic emotions, instincts and desires, is the *Nafs al-Ammarah*. Ammarah means *'ruling'*. All animals have a version of Nafs: just like with us, their Nafs is their toolkit for survival in nature, where morality and intelligence take second place over survival and victory. Animals act out of their Nafs alone, though some also have a degree of Intellect (intelligence). However, it is only us humans that have the self awareness that is in the Heart.

The Nafs is neither good nor bad. It is quite forceful, and is best dealt with in moderation and restraint. In this way, think of it like fire. Fire is a tool that we can use for many purposes, to cook, to warm us, to light the way, to illuminate the uncertain dark, and to defend ourselves, but also a dangerous force which can consume and destroy us if we do not respect and be careful with it.

The Nafs has a biological basis in how its functions are found and apparent, throughout the body. This is described by Islamic teachings; in science, functions of the Nafs have a close parallel with how emotions and instincts are rooted in the inner, lower parts of the brain, which in turn are connected very intimately to the rest of the body through nerves and hormones, making us *feel* emotions in quite a physical sense.

The Nafs is strong

The Nafs has a strong hold over us as human beings. It is filled with the impulses, strong emotions, and wishes to just do whatever we want. It is a very powerful force: if we are not mindful of it, it simply commands us, it dominates us. A person who just follows their Nafs mindlessly, does whatever they desire, without consideration of consequences or feeling any guilt.

Sometimes we are misled into doing whatever we desire without thinking it through properly; it is not a good way to be because we do not consider consequences, and we over-react. Afterwards we 'come to our senses' and we often realise that we we have done has been harmful to us or those around us.

Essentially, the Nafs is the collection of basic emotions, desires and instincts that we have in common with all living things. Our anger, our quest for pleasure, our sense of curiosity, our impulsive reactions to things, our sense of anxiety and insecurity, and even our tendency to be jealous of others who have status, power, or things that we want.

In common with other living things, the Nafs also has instincts and emotions which are socially oriented. In this way, it is like the ego. Our Nafs is insecure, leading us to show that we are strong, to exhibit strength to show value to others, or to scare off competitors. The Nafs is very loyal, helping us to bond with others regardless of their faults, sticking by them because they are part of our circle. We use the Nafs when we interpreting subtle cues from others, in their body language and facial expressions, to inform ourselves about how to act around them. This can be very useful, especially when they are behaving in a way that is inconsistent with what they are saying.

The Nafs also what leads us to try to be popular with everyone. We can be misled into very exhausting efforts to keep everyone happy, no matter the cost. Our Nafs leads us to worry a lot about what other people think, to the point where we are consumed by this insecurity. It leads us to value luxury, high status, and pride for the sake of showing off. Our Nafs is easily influenced: it makes us feel miserable if someone is critical of us.

Depending on our emotional state, the Nafs can also lead to being over- or under-confident. The Nafs does not think about consequences, and doesn't like planning things. It lives based on its past prejudices, suspicious assumptions, and seeks quick pleasures impatiently. When we do something wrong, our Nafs gets threatened, and we go to extremes, either denying any responsibility for the problem and blaming others, or taking too much responsibility for it, blaming ourselves entirely and completely collapsing under the weight of self-blame, not taking into account the other factors outside our control that could have led to the mistake.

It is our lifelong battle to manage the Nafs: to use it for good, for example to bond with others, energise ourselves, and conquer our difficulties, but also to manage the bad- to stop it from distracting us with emotion or from acting mindlessly or selfishly. Shaitan is most easily seen at work when he tempts us to act according the extremes of our Nafs.

The Intellect

A human acting with their Intellect is behaving by relying on their knowledge and logic.

How the Intellect works

We use our Intellect to figure out new things, and to solve problems, contemplate our actions, and plan and prepare for the future. The intellect works cooperatively with others, obeying your intentions by helping plan and organise your actions.

The Intellect works by seeking **evidence and truth.** As such, the Intellect works best when there is honesty, rules and laws, analysis, problem-solving, and self control.

The Intellect likes to **solve problems, and to achieve things by planning them out.** It is patient, and thinks of consequences before jumping to any decision. It is therefore a very useful thing, but it can be quite slow, and prone to over analysis and indecision if we don't use our judgment to act when we have enough information to act.

The social, interpersonal Intellect

The Intellect also has a social element, but different from the Nafs. Socially, our Intellect is keen to research, cooperate with others, and with obeying rules and laws that have been agreed upon or set. It takes people at their word, and gets confused and disappointed if others don't do what they say they would, or if thy break the rules.

Like the Nafs, the Intellect seeks to get along with others, but unlike the Nafs, your Intellect does not need approval to feel OK. The Intellect is more independent, being satisfied internally, allowing you to think for yourself. This is because the Intellect, if forced to choose, will choose truth over popularity. This may be morally better but can cause you trouble if you don't judge the situation properly: if you believe you are right when everyone else is wrong, it is often wiser to hold back on confronting them rather than arguing with a whole crowd.

The Intellect, unrestrained, would argue a point beyond its utility, and lose popularity as a result.

The Intellect enjoys Responsibility and Accountability

The Intellect is *internally satisfied.* With the Intellect, we are able to take responsibility for things that happen to us, and act proactively rather than reactively. We use our Intellect to deal with others based on their *actions and qualities,* unlike the Nafs, which as we learned earlier, judges based on quick impressions, appearance, attractiveness and other less tangible things.

A person acting with their Intellect looks for solutions and compromises, and endeavours to be fair and to act in a way that is in keeping with rules and laws.

The Intellect is weaker than the Nafs

Compared to the Nafs, the Intellect is slow to think and slow to respond. It is also weaker in terms of the influence it has over our actions: if we are very emotional, then our Intellect does not function well. The other problem with the Intellect is that it is very idealistic: a person acting with Intellect alone assumes that everyone will behave fairly and that good things happen if we do good things; in this way, it is a bit detached from the real world.

Intellect alone is not enough: we are in danger of missing out on the realities of what the world is like, and living in an over-simplified world blind to dangers and risks. Other people act emotionally, irrationally, out of their Nafs.

We need our Nafs to understand others' Nafs better: our Nafs is sensitive to others' feelings, so when we put it to good use, we can use the Nafs like an emotional sensor: we can feel what the other person is feeling, getting us an insight into their emotions.

Life is not always fair or understandable, and between intelligence and emotion, we are still lost in the material world. We need a higher purpose in life, and a sense of judgment as to when to act, how to act, and how to interpret our thoughts and feelings so as to make the best decisions and progress in life. This is where the Heart- our true self- comes in.

True Self Awareness: Your Heart

How you experience yourself right now, and the very reason you are reading this, is because of your conscious awareness: your Heart. Your Heart is the overseer of your thoughts and feelings, the final judge of your actions, and the guide as to your purpose in life. It is the very essence of who you are, and if you nurture it, it will help you towards whatever you want to achieve.

Your Heart can be weak or strong, depending on how you look after your intentions and actions. Your Heart is the seat of your your Deen, and your other roles and purposes in life. Your Heart is not strong on its own: it is something that, with modest and steady effort, can become the strongest part of your mind, even stronger than your Nafs. You will always have a Nafs; you are born with it. Your Intellect will develop depending on your natural strength, how confidently you pursue your curiosity for the world, and how well you use the opportunities that come your way.

The Heart on its own

You keep certain sacred things in your Heart, and would do well to pay them attention every day. These are your Deen, your Rules of Conduct, and your Truths of Life. More details on this later in this book.

Heart and Nafs

By using your Heart to understand your Nafs, you add temperance and understanding to your emotions. You become **emotionally intelligent**. Emotional intelligence is the capacity to be aware of, control, and express your emotions, and to handle interpersonal relationships with fairness and expertise as to how others are feeling.

Heart and Intellect

By using your Heart to direct your Intellect, you add purpose and meaning to your skills, abilities and your creativity. You become **wise and purposeful**.

Thus, the Heart will learn to work with the different parts of your mind as assets, working around your weaknesses.

A well trained Heart makes life easier to get through. The more you use your awareness, the more you can go through life dealing with everyday issues on 'automatic navigation' getting through things easily and peacefully.

What is in our Heart is the truest reflection of our best self: the best of our emerging personality and characteristics as human beings. If we don't pay attention to it, it will tend to run according to whichever is the more powerful out of the Nafs or the Intellect. Neither is particularly effective on its own.

Alhamdulillah, when we are truly mindful and wise, we use our Heart to make the final judgments and decisions about what to do about any given situation, and we act with firmness of purpose. If we do not look after ourselves then the Heart is weak, and our true self never comes out: instead, we become beholden to the wild whims of the Nafs, or we are lost and lacking in warmth, in blindly relying on a misguided Intellect.

We therefore need to nurture our Heart. We can do so if we look what makes for the things that make for good conscious awareness:

- Remembering Allah.
- Attending closely to our roles in life, both towards other people and to our own aims and goals.
- Seeking out constructive and helpful lessons from whatever experiences we have.
- Paying attention to what is important in our thoughts and feelings, because we become more aware of ourselves and more able to supervise our own actions.

A strong Heart is able to deal with life very efficiently and effortlessly, seeing off temptation and attending to our goals and needs in a contented way. Allah judges us on our actions, and on what we have put into our Heart.

The Heart, carefully attended to as we go through life, with its wisdom, deen, and its knowledge, will get us through life easily and without fuss.

The Heart is able to act like a monitor: we can use it to search and observe our minds, so that we can decode the emotions and feelings from the Nafs, and direct our Intellect towards solving problems, being cooperative, living within the law, and planning and implementing good and worthy deeds.

Paid proper attention, the Heart is stronger and quicker than both the Nafs and the Intellect. It is therefore, potentially, the strongest of all our mental forces.

The Heart can become misguided, and we can correct it

The Heart can be thought of as a sort of knowledge base and guidance for both emotional and intellectual things, and when we train it properly we can become wiser and find ways of getting through challenges that come up repetitively. To see what is meant, read on.

When we go through anything in life, we can either

- experience it but be mentally absent, preoccupied with anxieties or concerns or distracted with meaningless or troubling things which we cannot do anything about, or
- experience it fully, from moment to moment, so that we can do makes best of whatever is going on in front of us at the time

Clearly, the difference between the two things is important. This difference is the purpose of a strong and peaceful Heart: guiding our awareness to be fully attendant to what is going on, and setting aside concerns or distractions that are not controllable.

Similarly, when we experience anything in life, we form a memory of it. What happens to that memory? We can

- forget about it
- remember it passively, letting the memory of it just settle in the mind unexamined, or
- use the memory, reflecting on it to question what the facts really were, and would be helpful next time round, gaining experience and knowledge.

Again, the Heart is the difference: we can enhance our own intelligence about life if we pay closer attention to our experiences, reflecting on them, discovering wisdoms about ourselves and the world around us that we would not have done had we just carried on unquestioningly. Often we form memories and attitudes that are wrong, because we haven't properly examined ourselves.

Many of us go through lives with entirely the wrong attitude toward something, because we let the memory of it form without properly questioning it. For example, we might believe that people of a certain race are more selfish, because we were told as such by someone, or because we had a single bad experience with someone who happened to be of that race.

This is unhelpful to us; we have dismissed an entire people because of prejudice- something the Prophet (PBUH) warned us against in

his last sermon. Using your own awareness, you can reflect on your experiences with less emotions, think about the guidance that your Deen gives you, and come to a wiser conclusion- that relying on others' prejudices, or a single bad experience, is not a good method to understand an entire people.

It really is no more magical than that: simple reflection, if you think about it, is massively helpful: we can completely rewrite our character with greater depth and better conduct, if we take time to nurture what is in our Heart: remember Allah, pay attention to life in a more present way, and take time to pay attention to our conduct and our beliefs, making sure that these things are correct and strong. Our Nafs and Intellect are both calmer, more accessible, and easier to guide and understand as a result. We get closer to our best self. This is the benefit and beauty of a strong Heart.

We are born with the Nafs. The Intellect develops over time; the Heart comes a little later than Nafs and Intellect, and it is higher and more influential than either, if we take the time to nurture it. The more we develop it, the easier it gets.

The mind is a body part just like any other, but being invisible, we tend to assume it is the same in one person to the next. The reality is people are very different indeed.

The best of us are those who make constant effort to be mindful of our conduct, and attend to our loved ones and obligations as best we can. Nurturing your Heart, making time to understand and work with your intelligence and with your emotions, will inshallah make this path easy for us.

When the Nafs and the Intellect are satisfied and properly understood, they operate in sync with the Heart. Alhamdulillah, the mind is our most powerful tool, and it is very responsive to attention and care. We get out what we put in.

Being an effective person

Alhamdulillah, we have both the gift and the burden of free will, therefore we must take responsibility for ourselves in everything we do. We must take responsibility for whatever feelings we have, and for any decisions we make. Only then do we gain some sense of our own power to change things for the better.

The biggest and most constant danger we face is giving in to impulsive thinking, fleeting desires, seeking meaningless prizes and quick pleasures. Time and time again people look at what they have and devalue it, wanting more power, and craving the things that they lack, just because they lack them. They avoid making effort to discover helpful truths and productive conduct. Much of this comes from having little control and understanding over the Nafs.

Too many people do this in the world today. When we are not mindful, it could be said that Shaitan leads us astray by preying on the extremes and whims of the Nafs.

We fail to remember that being helpful to others, and remembering Allah's guidance, are the two routes to success and contentment. We end up not learning anything, being selfish and prejudiced, and being excluded or ignored by others because we fail to put others' needs before our own. It is a sad, destructive and wasteful life.

You are never your best self: the most you can do is try

You, in your truest version of yourself, must try to work towards your best. This is all you need to do. Achieving perfection is not possible, nor is it the aim. *The effort to be your best* is what counts. The result is in the hands of Allah.

In other words, it is your job to simply try your best to act in a way that is mindful of the higher wisdoms and purposes you have, and you are attentive to what is going on in front of you, acting in the best way you can at at any given time. This takes effort and humility.

If you do develop yourself in this way, you will be more successful in avoiding the dangers of acting according to the Nafs alone, and you will be able to make balanced and fair decisions, and live with other people in a healthy and fulfilled way, achieving the things you set out to do.

Nobody conquers their Nafs all the time, nor is anybody fully in control of their actions. We just keep trying, humbly and studiously. This is easier once you apply yourself to looking after your mind and your actions using the knowledge and methods described in this book. It is a constant effort that you must make.

To be a good person means really to be at peace with the laws of human decency, to respect other people, to have good relationships with others, and to pursue good things in the path of your life. This is not just true of Muslims- all the great religions have this as their basis. Islam has the most elegant way of describing the lifelong battle to be good and righteous, acting

above and beyond our base instincts, using good conduct, intelligence, and Deen to be as good as we can be. We as people must be vigilant over our desires, and become more in tune with the highest version of ourselves, at peace with our obligations and our aims, both for material purposes and for the sake of doing what Allah has asked of us.

Essentially, the fulfilled and wise person has a Heart that is sympathetic to both their Nafs and their Intellect, keeping both in check, and addressing the needs of both, whilst also striving towards matters of *deen and dunya:* faith and the material world.

REFLECTIONS

We are all puppets in the hands of power;
Power which we need to recognise is actually our own.

A well educated mind is not full: it is open.

Don't ask a child *what* they want to be
when they grow up.
Ask them *how* they want to be.

Maturity is achieved when you realise that all of life
Will have stress and tension to some measure.

If all you do is go from A to B,
You will miss all the other letters of the alphabet.

The Nafs loves to trick the body into believing
It must carry the burden of its worries.

Tension is who you think you should be.
Relaxation is who you are.

Allah designed the body very well.
You can neither pat your back, nor kick yourself, very
easily.

You don't need to be what people call you;
It's who you answer to that counts.

INSTANT INSIGHTS

Chapter 3: The Nafs

Alhamdulillah. Praises are due to Allah for giving us the Nafs. It is a part of us that Allah has invested us with for good reason. Without it, we would probably not survive. The Nafs is our most basic form of thinking: it is the seat of our emotions. it is a strong force, which we must learn to understand, if we are not to be overpowered by it.

The Nafs is the most primitive part of your mind, and is mostly non-verbal. That is to say, it doesn't rely on language and logic: instead, it is the collection of emotions, feelings and instincts that we have in common with other animals. It is both useful and destructive.

Think of the Nafs as a bit like fire. Fire has its qualities as a tool, weapon and hazard. Emotions and instincts are the same. In a primitive way, the Nafs is driven to react to things extremely, and doesn't stop to ask questions. Whatever the Nafs wants, it wants NOW. Fire can be both useful and dangerous. It can warm us, keep us close together, and we can use its light to see in the dark, to alert us to the things our eyes wouldn't otherwise see. But if we don't respect fire, it can hurt us. It can burn us, it can grow out of control, and destroy our lives.

The Nafs in a simple picture

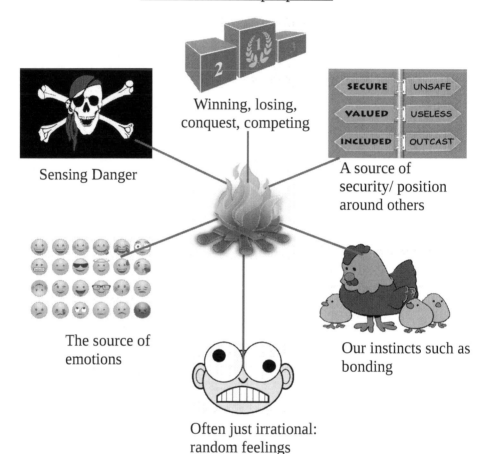

Sensing Danger

Winning, losing, conquest, competing

A source of security/ position around others

The source of emotions

Our instincts such as bonding

Often just irrational: random feelings

If it were a creature, the Nafs would be a bit like a primitive cave-dweller: not too clever, rather basic, and neither good nor bad, the cave-dweller behaves in a way that ensures his or her survival in his or her primitive group. It can be cautious, loyal, aggressive, frightened, aggressive, bold, cautious, easily frightened, and quick to anger and fight.

The Nafs senses very quickly, using feelings and estimations

Your Nafs understands the world through impressions and feelings, which show up as our emotions, and instincts. These can be helpful; it is the feeling you get when you judge someone by appearance or facial expression: it could be correct, but it is often wrong. It is prone to prejudice and mistakes. Your Nafs is also powerful: emotions are generally able to overpower our Intellect. Take this example. Supposing we were walking along and came across a lion:

Your Nafs is primed to react rapidly with fear and caution: we would instinctively make efforts to hide or escape. This is of course a very useful and appropriate instinct. Were we to rely only on the Intellect, we would be still trying to figure out what to do, looking at the lion as simply an animal, without our instinct: without that inborn sense of danger. Acting on Intellect alone, we would remain standing, making pointless efforts to work out irrelevant things such as if the lion were young or old, hungry or not, and what have you. Clearly this would not help us deal with the grave danger that the lion actually presents!

A lion is a wild animal with a predatory appearance: we are programmed at a very biological level, to be afraid of these things, and act on this fear by instinctively hiding or escaping. Even a newborn baby shows a fear response when shown an image of an animal with sharp teeth. This fear is encoded in the DNA. This is the miracle of the Nafs.

How the Nafs inhabits the body

Science has brought considerable knowledge and theory to explain the Nafs as part of the body. We can see how the emotional centres are particularly centred in the lower and inner parts of the brain, and these regions are connected to the rest of the body, including upwards to the higher parts of the brain (logic, consciousness) and downwards, to every organ from head to toe.

We can observe clear signs of the emotional state in everything from the size of the pupil in the eye, to our facial expressions, body language, and even the rate at which we digest food and sweat from our skin.

The Nafs is connected to the body through nerves and hormones, which communicate and relay messages about our physical state to and from the brain. Activation of the body makes us more ready to respond to threats or circumstances. Nowadays, we are in a world where we even though we mostly don't face life threatening circumstances, we still react emotionally with the same way to stress.

When our emotions run high, we can notice the following things:

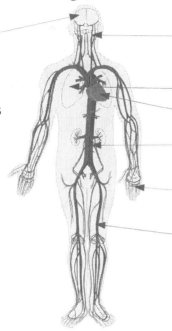

Reduced blood flow to logical and rational areas: mind goes blank.

Increased blood flow to emotional areas:
Anxiety, anger, arousal

Breathing rate higher
Heart rate higher

Butterflies in the stomach

Sweating

More blood flow to muscles: they are readier to go into action.

- Blood flow to the emotional regions increases, making emotions get stronger.
- Blood flow to the upper areas of the brain- where logic and language reside- is actually decreased, making us lose the capacity to think things through properly, and feel 'lost for words'.
- Heart rate and breathing rate go up. We feel our heart pumping, and our breathing gets shallow and rapid.
- Blood flow to the gut decreases, giving us a feeling of butterflies.
- Bloodflow to the muscles increases, giving us the feeling of nervous energy.

The Nafs is there since birth

We are born with the Nafs; it almost completely dominates the feelings and behaviour of infants and small children.

If a small child wants something, they want it immediately. They are not able to think about the consequences; for example, they will gladly eat sweets or their favourite snack until they get sick, time and time again.

They are extremely emotional, getting both very happy, and very upset, over relatively inconsequential things. They are not aware of others' desires: they think only about what they need.

Equally though, their Nafs drives them to show bonding to their parents, to show rivalry and love for their siblings; and to be curious and playful about the world around them.

Different people have a different 'styles' of Nafs, meaning that people show different amounts of different emotional and instinctive tendencies.

Temperament: your individual emotional blueprint

Each of us is born with a 'temperament' which is a pattern of ways in which any given person, even a small child, reacts to things emotionally. Temperament refers to things such as how settled or anxious a child is in general, how attached they are to their parent, how they cope with separation, and so on. Different basic temperaments are observed, even in newborns, and it is true to say that these traits are often observed even when we become adults. A person's basic 'temperament' can be anxious, secure, or detached, and so on.

With our children, we must be sympathetic to their Nafs, dealing with them in a way that encourages them to calm themselves, and to start to use their Intellect and Heart once they are capable of doing so. Children can be very good at getting what they want, because they appeal to our emotions- our own Nafs.

Alhamdulillah, this is part of the miracle of our design as human beings. The sound of a baby crying is universally effective in drawing attention and sympathy from parents, causing them to find it difficult to concentrate on whatever they are doing. This is a good example of how the Nafs has its uses in guiding us to take care of the ones we love over and above our worldly preoccupations.

The Nafs can dominate over your thinking for two reasons

1. It is very strong: more powerful than Intellect.
2. It is very rapid, quicker than Intellect.

This is why we need the Heart: when we nurture and educate ourselves in our Heart, we can eventually gain better control over it, but many people don't embark on this exercise properly: their Nafs remains their strongest and quickest mental force.

Friend or foe?	The Nafs sizes someone up quickly, based on appearance.
Good food or not?	The Nafs judges by smell and taste alone.
Good purchase or not?	The Nafs judges based on how much you have been influenced by advertising, social media or celebrities.
Trustworthy person?	The Nafs judges based on how much the person is smiling or making eye contact.

Many times these decisions are correct, but often they are not at all right. When you are emotionally charged, your whole body reacts: heart rate goes up, you get sweaty, your breathing rate goes up. When our emotions are charged, it becomes very difficult to challenge your Nafs because the blood supply to your Intellect- seated in the frontal outer parts of your brain- is physically reduced, diverted to the lower emotional centres where the Nafs is in control. You lose the ability to think logically when you are emotionally consumed.

We have the Nafs in common with animals: we become emotionally heightened when we imagine or face a threat. Animals survive by escaping, or fighting (the so called 'flight or fight' response)- and we have this too. Impulses and rapid, mindless reactions to the environment help us survive the most dangerous of threats, or to manage conflict by fighting or escaping it.

The Nafs doesn't use words and language: it is 'non-verbal'

Emotions don't feel 'conscious' or logical. They are mostly non-verbal, meaning they don't rely on words and language. This is why we can't understand or talk about them as easily as we would like to: we literally can't 'access' the language parts of the brain easily when we are very emotionally charged.

When someone says they are 'lost for words' this is because they are so emotionally shocked by something, there is literally less blood flowing to their Intellect- where language is found. As a result, their language becomes more basic, and they don't exercise control over it, saying things they don't mean and exaggerating things to suit their point of view, without even knowing they are doing so.

When you see, hear or think about something, the messages go to your Intellect, and your Nafs. However, the Nafs is quicker to react: emotional centres process messages more quickly and generate responses more quickly. This is why people talk about 'acting without thinking', doing something impulsively out of strong emotion because they literally have not actually begun to think about their actions in a more logical, calmer way. It is no surprise that afterwards the same people get confused about why they acted in some way: they don't have the words or the memory to explain what happened.

The Nafs is active, whether you are aware of it or not

That is to say, emotions are mostly *involuntary*. We can't help our feelings and emotions about things. They come because the Nafs is constantly appraising the information we receive from the outside world, or when we are thinking about some new problem or old memory. The Nafs makes decisions about these things in a very rapid way, because in part at least, just like in animals, the Nafs is interested in keeping you alive, and in easy opportunities to get ahead. The Nafs has, at is root, a survival instinct.

Some people are very aware of their Nafs. This gives them the chance to keep the Nafs in check by taking their feelings into account when making decisions. But this is not always the case: some people who are fully aware of their Nafs still let it dominate their decisions and actions anyway, perhaps because the life they lead means they find more use to certain things that the Nafs is skilled at, for example fighting or greed.

People who lack insight into their emotions are basically unaware that their Nafs is a part of them that they must engage with and control. These people can go wrong in one of two ways:

a) *They are either dominated by their Nafs,* and so they are very reactive and emotionally all over the place.
b) *They shut the Nafs out, becoming cold and isolated*. They live their lives only with a cold kind of detachment from their emotions, missing danger, missing social life, and unaware of why they feel their emotions.

Even very intelligent people, who have great Intellect, can become so focussed on one part of a problem that they miss the bigger picture, and lack common sense. They only get 'caught out' by their Nafs when they end up doing something totally rash and out of character, when the ignored Nafs just lets go of all that pressure at once.

The Nafs in the big wide world

The Nafs shows itself in other ways, depending on the situation. For example, think about when people are in crowds or large groups. The Nafs, like all creatures, has a strong connection to groups: it is what drives people to want to be part of group, and leads them to behave in a way that confirms and reassures their group and themselves that they belong. When all the people in a group do this, they show loyalty and strength, but when it goes wrong, they often react more emotionally and often more extremely than any one of them would do if they were alone.

53

How the emotions and instincts of Nafs communicate with us

Basically, it's like this: we *over-react to everything*. Your Nafs tells you what is going on using strong emotions, provocative imagined scenarios, and gut feelings, all of which come very quickly, tempting you to over-react, and not to think more logically using reason, wisdom or higher judgment.

If you feel giddy excitement, it means your Nafs is anticipating something good happening. Fear means that the Nafs is telling us to be ready to fight or run away. Anger happens when your Nafs feels let down if you feel belittled or ignored, or if you lose in a conflict, or fail at something.

All of these emotions have a place: anger is an antidote to pain, and gives us a motivation to learn from our mistakes. Fear is what we need when we need to escape from a bad situation. In our daily lives, it is true to say that these emotions, though useful, are always too strong. And when they are strong, they get in the way of making more calm, sensible decisions: we forget our moral codes, fail to think about consequences.

Thankfully, most of us in the world do not face immediate threats of death, and are not embroiled in life-threatening conflicts. For those of us who do, their Nafs is able to guide their survival, giving them instincts and alertness through its worst parts. May Allah makes their lives peaceful, Ameen.

What kind of Nafs do you have?

Although we all have a Nafs, your Nafs could be very different from mine in terms of its particular preoccupations. Each Nafs, from person to person, has its own 'dominant drives' from a big list of many different drives. Take the example of Ali. Ali is extremely competitive, wanting to prove himself better against others in his school class. His brother Adam is more relaxed, and more interested in making friends with other people in the class, letting competition take a back seat. And so on and so forth.

Not only this, but we also show different parts of our Nafs depending on how we feel, what we are thinking, where we are, who we are with, and what we are doing.

Take the example of Sarah. Sarah is in an elevator, going up to visit a friend in an apartment building. Suddenly the elevator stops; it seems stuck. Sarah becomes anxious, almost panicking. The situation seems hopeless, but a few minutes later it gets working again and she is relieved. She reflects on how anxious she became.

Then on another day, Sarah is in the same elevator, but this time she has her two little sisters with her; they are only 3 and 5 years old. The elevator gets stuck, but Sarah does not get anxious: she immediately turns to her sisters, trying to give them comfort and reassurance; she even notices that there is an emergency button: she didn't even see that last time.

When the lift gets moving again, Sarah reflects on how she was almost a different person: this happened because her emotions were preoccupied with a strong drive to comfort her smaller siblings; her own fears were set aside. It is astonishing how well the Nafs can be adapted to different situations without our even knowing.

The irrationality of the Nafs

The Nafs is also plainly 'irrational' at times. When we are just waking up, or very tired, the Nafs can throw up feelings unpredictably. We might not understand them or even know why they are there at all: this is just part of the nature of the Nafs. When this happens, it is better to think not about why we are emotional, but to focus on how to just move ahead without reacting to our emotions.

It can be confusing for a child or young person when they have large swings in mood or unexplained bursts of anger or sadness, without any good reason as to why they are feeling it.
At this point, it is useful to remind them that this is part of the nature of emotions to be sometimes unexplained, and frequently too excessive. This explanation is often a great help just on its own.

The many instincts and drives that can be found in the Nafs.

With guidance from science and from Islamic teaching, we discover that many of the instincts we are told about are embedded within us in a way that is written into our DNA.

The table over the next three pages describes some of the many different features and functions the Nafs could be said to have.

Drive/instinct	What is it?	What does it want?	Too much of it leads to what?
Love for your spouse	To be with a single mate, and overlook their faults	**Loyalty and parenthood** Sticking with a partner through thick and thin.	Implosion. A poor choice of partner means you get hurt and can't see the truth
Victory	To feel on top of situations	**Dominance.** Pride; the energy and wish to see things through	Selfishness. Aggressiveness, arrogance; not dealing with inevitable losses that will come your way
Parenting/nurturing	Looking after yours or others' young	**Legacy.** Satisfying the need to raise the future members of a group.	Exhaustion. Dominated by parent role at the expense of one's health or wellbeing. Making a poor choice of partner.
Gentle physical contact and ca	Grooming and taking care of others	**Bonding.** Increases trust, loyalty and cooperation	Intrusion. Invading others' space and privacy; making others uncomfortable by this action
Sibling rivalry	Play-fighting; challenging siblings	**Practice.** Building physical strength and social skills	Unnecessary violence. Destructive or harmful competition

Different features and functions that can be said to come from the Nafs

Drive/ instinct	What is it?	What does it want?	Too much of it leads to what?
Safety	To avoid taking chances	**Survival.** Prevents you from being hurt or wasting time	Stagnation. Fear of any change. Always losing out on opportunities which could help you.
Status/ respect	To be clear, preferably higher up, in where you you. You have clarity of role in the group. fit in.	**Respect.** Other people respect with status and rank, to the expense of allies.	Loneliness. Needless conflict or obsession
Possession	To have things which denote wealth or status	**Certainty and status** Other people respect you and ally with you. Protection from poverty.	Isolation. Targeted by jealous people. Hoarding things beyond actual need. Selfishness.
Partnering/ companions	To be with a close companion	**Assistance.** Having another person share responsibilities and skills. Protection.	Exploitation. Being vulnerable or needy. Being exploited by those pretending to be your friend.
Belonging	Being part of the tribe	**Protection.** Strong identity. Combining efforts with others.	Exhaustion. Frantic efforts to please or prove your worth at the expense of your own dignity or sanity.

Different features and functions that can be said to come from the Nafs (contd)

Drive/ instinct	What is it?	What does it want?	Too much of it leads to what?
Gossip and rumour	Using emotions and prejudices to create or exaggerate a story	**Warning.** Maintaining or enhancing the reputation of a strong figure, or protecting the group from a bad person without needing the full facts.	Damage. To others' lives or reputations, or to your own life or reputation, as a result of inaccurate or plainly untrue stories.
Extreme decisions (too cautious, or the opposite: something too risky)	Being too cautious, or the opposite- too negative, about facts are unclear; helps to increase commitment and confidence in a group situation	**Certainty.** Makes for clarity where something; making a bad judgment someone or something	Falsehood. Overlooking the truth about overcommitting energy towards something or someone, not based on truth.
Negative salience	Focussing on the chances of a bad outcome, however small.	**Survival.** You only fall off a big cliff once. Nafs believes that avoiding risk is more important than reward.	Anxiety. Paranoia. Mistrust. Indecision. Obsessiveness. Being manipulated by others who preach or exaggerate fear. Favour safety, fearing change.

60

The Nafs in different sexes

We have learnt that different people have different emotional outlooks. Alhamdulillah, more than this, Allah has designed men and women to be broadly different too. In other words, men and women have different emotional drives and instincts. This does not mean that we are entirely different from each other. It simply means that we have been given different amounts of this or that quality, in order to better serve our roles in human society.

A word of caution: it is not right to say that males only think in a male way and females only in a female way: what we know its that some people can have greater amounts of different qualities. Both men and women have qualities which overlap one another's. Alhamdulillah, Allah has given us all different degrees of things, probably so that we all find a niche in our community that we can fulfil.

The male Nafs tends to favour being strong and offering security. The male Nafs is concerned with making sure that other people know what is his property, and with making sure that the people he cares for are safe. Taken too far, a man can become very petty over small boundary issues, or seeing the people he cares for as his 'property' too. You might see when male animals fight each other for 'possession' of a group of females. Unfortunately, this is still done by people. Allah has discouraged men from treating anyone else as property.

Islam has always discouraged treating women as property, giving women rights to have their own property and independence at a time when this was a very new and controversial concept.

Similarly, slavery is also deeply frowned upon. Men must understand their Nafs and acknowledge that they have a duty to look after the people that they care for, but to not see them as property to be traded or used in any way.

The male is also prouder than the female, tending to blame other people when things go wrong, rather than blaming himself. As a general guide, men tend to become more angry when they are upset, blaming an external source, while women tend to become sad, blaming themselves. Perhaps men need anger to fuel their determination, but it should not be more than this: expressing anger is one of the most sinful acts we can do.

Alhamdulillah, like this and in so many other instances, we learn how the Nafs has positive qualities if taken in moderation, which become troublesome if we let them run loose.

The female Nafs is adept at reading emotions, and being socially aware. This is clearly a useful force, but uncontrolled, it could lead to gossiping and emotional manipulation. The female Nafs is also very nurturing and nesting. It gives women the drive to have and look after their children, and to create and maintain a comfortable home environment: the 'woman's touch', as it were.

Again, this overlaps with the male wish to create a safe home, and having a good eye for design is neither the exclusive domain of men nor women.

The female Nafs is more likely to seek to depend on the male, maintaining a strong social bond between husband and wife. However, if this gets out of control the female sees the male as a source of all self esteem, becoming dependent on the man to the point of helplessness, or manipulating the male emotionally to get him to pay her more attention.

These qualities are not hard and fast; men and women do share many similar qualities. Men can be nurturing and caring, and women can be aggressive. Indeed, some people might have high amounts of both: maleness and femaleness are not opposite sides of a scale. Rather, they are independent qualities, and people are individuals. Whichever elements of Nafs occur in you, they are yours: get to know them and accept them, making the best of them without letting them become destructive or excessive.

The Nafs in Children

In children, we need to deal with the Nafs with warmth and patience, and nurture their Intellect and Heart gently and consistently.

Small children are dominated by their Nafs, above all else. They are perceptive to our emotions even if we think they are not noticing.

Our main job with children is to nurture and love them, while knowing that their Nafs is dominating their actions and decisions when they are little. They do not have fully developed Intellects, and their Heart itself is yet to form its moral views, outlook on life, or spiritual outlook.

Our aim is to be sympathetic to the child's Nafs, calming and reassuring it for its need of love and authority, while alongside

this, we introduce and demonstrate Intellect (reasoning and rules, and practice) and Heart (morality, faith, and self awareness) both systematically when we talk to them at bedtime or over food, and opportunistically when there are incidents or dilemmas that crop up.

We cannot expect children to think intellectually or morally very early on, but we can introduce these concepts to them as they grow. By the time they are six to nine years old, they will have a decent amount of Intellect and a basic understanding of self awareness and morality. Thus, the early years are good opportunities for us to set them up well with lessons and examples of good rules and conduct, and awareness of Allah. It is normal for children to cry, to be needy, fussy, selfish or impatient. It is unwise for us to punish them or scold them for this: it is better, first and foremost, to consider that they don't know any different just yet, and to seek to change this behaviour in a calm and effective way rather than letting our own emotions get the better of us.

The child, like the adult, learns best when it is calm and curious: this is best done by settling their Nafs rather than frightening it. Giving them hugs, love and reassurance that we are there for them comes first, must be done frequently and without restraint. Once we settle the Nafs like this, we can then introduce reasons and rules(Intellect), and morality (Heart).

We should be unafraid of being firm: the child's Nafs does seek and respond to authority, but we should do so in a warm and benevolent way, explaining our reasons for setting boundaries.

Consequences vs punishment

It is wiser to use consequences rather than punishment. The difference between these two things is important. Consequences are designed to teach maturity and sense, in calm emotion. Punishment is intended to create negative emotion. The desire to punish comes from the Nafs; we punish when we are desperate, or when we lack the imagination to change someone's behaviour in a more effective way.

Punishment is similar to vengeance in that it seeks to make the recipient suffer emotionally or physically. This may work, frightening the person into submission, but it rarely has a long-lasting effect: used repeatedly, it only leads to fear and resentment. As soon as the punisher's back is turned, the child feels free to reoffend.

As it grows, the child would learn to lie, or not control their own actions. Worse still, the child could go pass on the punishment, hurting people they have power over..

Consequences, on the other hand, come from the Intellect. Intellect relies on reasons, rules and goals. Rules are there because they are the way to be a good person. Following rules leads to good consequences, while breaking them leads to an absence of the good consequences and a reminder to follow the rules.

We should not wait until a child does something bad to then interact with it. This would mislead them into thinking we are only interested when they do something wrong. We must pay attention to them, frequently and foremost, for the good things they do. It is important to actively look for when the child does anything the right way, and praise them and reward them at those times. When a child breaks the rules, we must seek to understand their reasons, encourage them to truth, and remind them of the rules. No need to resort to extremes as a routine: this just creates fear.

All the while, we must nurture the child's Nafs by giving plenty of physical contact or reassurance- whatever seems to settle the child in a comfortable way, helping it feel cared for and loved unconditionally.

Asking the child to help draw up the rules is a very good technique: it gives the child the opportunity to think about the reasons for rules, and the morality and basis for good behaviour.

Of course, punishment has its place, particularly when there is a grave danger that the child's repeated misdemeanours could lead to harm or danger. For example, if a child repeatedly runs out in the road, and doesn't seem to respond to explanation, then a reasonable punishment might be to immediately deny the child any further treats, and to talk to them very sternly indeed: expressing a measured amount of anger would be appropriate in order to instil a small amount of fear in their Nafs: after all, getting run over is a mortal danger, and children are not always able to act reasonably because their intellect is not yet developed enough to understand the danger, and they don't yet have the full ability to inhibit their desires to play or act impulsively. We all should have a degree of fear about things which endanger our lives, but we as parents need to underline the dangers that a child is not aware of.

If we do resort to punishment, it should be accompanied with explanation and reassurance, and it should be short lived and quick. The explanation is that it was for the child's protection, and we must always, all the while, give the child reassurance that we love the child: this is absolutely essential.

It would also be crucial to pay attention to the child when it does follow the rules: encouragement and reward of following the rules is far more likely to create a happy and confident child, rather than only interacting with the child significantly when he or she does something wrong.

"He took my ice cream!"

Adam takes his sister's ice cream from her hand. He is a child: he wants, so he takes. As a parent, you might get annoyed about it; your temptation is to shout at him. This is your own Nafs getting riled up. Being able to recognise when your own emotions are running high is crucial: you cannot act rationally or calmly when this is happening. It is best first to calm yourself, and only then act to help Adam and his sister out.

Children model themselves on how we act: if we use shouting and violence, then why would we expect them to learn any different? If a child is shouting too much, it is futile to shout at it to get it to change its behaviour. Isn't it better to show them how to handle our own emotions when they get out of hand? Tell them when you are upset and when you want to feel better or be on your own, and reassure them that they are not the source of your being upset: children's Nafs are very insecure, and will blame themselves otherwise, setting them up for undue guilt and anxiety.

Never blame the child for your being upset. You are responsible for your emotions and the emotions of the child, but the child is not responsible for your emotions.

Emotions lead a thinking person to use their senses,
but lead the unthinking person astray.

People who lack good character show it
by pointing out vices in others.

Those who demand recognition for their good deeds
should demand punishment for their vices too.

Acceptance of life, and admitting one's qualities:
the first steps towards personal growth.

Isn't it strange how seldom we gossip
about other peoples' secret virtues?

The rich and powerful cry that their vices are errors;
the errors of the poor are called crimes.

Resisting temptation is difficult for many people
because they don't want to discourage it completely.

The finest joys in life happen when there is
a degree of discipline and restraint to them.

We might be delivered from temptation,
but temptation keeps in touch with us all the same.

INSTANT INSIGHTS

Chapter 4: The Intellect

The word 'Intellect' means your ability to think for yourself, to use logic, to find truth, and to apply yourself to life's challenges. Basically, this means your intelligence. Different people have different types of intelligence in different amounts, but it all serves the same basic function: to become good at solving problems, to plan things, make them happen, and working within the rules and expectations that we have set for ourselves.

Your intellect is a good balancing force in your life: it can help give your ideas the planning and execution to achieve the goals that you might have, be they from your Nafs or from your Heart.

 The areas of our intelligence are found in the upper, outer parts of the brain, known as the neocortex and frontal lobes.

Think of the Intellect as your ability to solve problems and think things through, and your repository of abilities that help you to grow skills in whatever roles you have in life. You use the Intellect to learn, to create, and to improve your knowledge and skills. It is of great service to you in this way.

The Intellect thinks in a way that is systematic:
- Very logical, thinking through in a step-by-step way.
- Wanting to be clear about the actual facts and evidence of a situation, rather than opinions or feelings.
- Being fair and polite in treating others, even if it means coming to harm or upsetting important people.
- Caring a lot about doing things in the right way.

The weaknesses of the Intellect are:
- Not designed to work well when strong emotions are present, such as love, hate, fear, sadness, or elation.
- Unaware of danger: an untrained Intellect would go up to a lion in the same way it would approach a household cat.
- Often missing non-verbal things, like facial expressions or body language.
- Being overwhelmed and unable to find a solution when there are too many options.
- Becoming obsessed with things that are not easily fixed.

With your Intellect, you get a pleasant sense of satisfaction from:
- Doing something in the right way, without distractions
- Being patient, waiting for something, delaying gratification until the payoff or final reward.
- Abiding by the rules and laws.
- Being stuck into a project to approach, plan and carry out.
- Completing a project you wanted to see through to the end
- Collaborating with others to get something useful done.
- Help others without needing to be recognised or rewarded for it.

Qualities of the Intellect

Quality	What is it?	How it helps	When it goes wrong, or doesn't work
Logic	Step by step reasoning	**Solving** Working through problems in a focussed, progressive way	**Obliviousness** Missing the point when there is something more urgent or more important happening
Simple Morality	Knowing, or working out, right and wrong oneself	**Upstanding** Keeping to a code of conducting oneself	**Excessive Guilt** Being obsessed with rightness or wrongness beyond what is helpful.
Factual	Being focussed on seeking facts or figures	**Accuracy** More accurate knowledge and solutions	**Overloading** Gathering facts beyond usefulness; unable to make decisions as a result.
Equitable	Fairness and politeness	**Social Ease** Being kind and rational in decisions and interactions	**Vulnerability** Life, and other people, don't act fairly. Kindness becomes a kind of weakness.
Methodical	Doing things in a predictable, repetitive way	**Consistency** Predictable methods should bring predictable success	**Inflexibility** Being unable to adapt to changing world, or circumvent new problems
Planning	Preferring to map out things before doing them	**Efficiency** Using what you have in a productive and sustainable way	**Paralysis** Being too complicated and elaborate; not getting going

The Intellect is interested in facts, solving problems, and looking at things in a neutral way. This is very useful and has helped human beings to be inventive, adaptable, and more able to deal with complex issues like cooperating together, becoming skilled at a profession or trade, and learning how to create rules and systems, and learning how to discover new and better ways of achieving things.

The Intellect requires more conscious effort than the Nafs

The Intellect demands a lot of your conscious effort. It is not as strong or as quick as the Nafs. This is because it takes effort to gather proper facts and evidence, and to think about things in a deeper way. The Nafs uses the language of feelings and instincts which arrive quickly and are very compelling; solutions offered by the Nafs are typically very emotional, and rapid, and easy to follow through with. You could easily make the wrong decision. This Intellect is better at getting to the truth, and therefore at getting better quality decisions.

As an example, suppose there is a man, Adam, who is a trader and looking to buy some new fabric for his clothing factory. He is going to meet with a new person to see what kind of goods he has. The new person, Paul, arrives at the meeting place, and Adam sees that this man looks a little dirty and worn out. Adam makes up his mind quickly that this Paul is not to be worked with; he hears Paul out but doesn't pay attention. He promises to get back to Paul and then leaves, with no intention of actually following up.

If Adam had paid attention, he could have discovered that Paul had had a very long journey and the airline had lost his baggage. Paul was in fact a very good person to deal with, and his stock was extremely good too. Adam missed out.

The Intellect is a balancing force, in a way, often coming up with different, or even totally opposite advice than the Nafs.

The Nafs leads us to judge people by appearance and first impressions. This might be right in many cases, but not when we are properly trying to get to know someone. The Intellect is more interested in a person for their qualities and actions than in their appearances.

The Intellect is not always wise to the ways of the world

'Surely then, we should not need to take care of our appearance?' you might cry. The world is not like this. In considering how we come across to others, we would be wisest to consider both Nafs and Intellect: dressing properly and keeping a good appearance is a strong sunnah from the Prophet, as is using things like fragrances and gifts to endear us to people both new and familiar. This calms their Nafs, they spend time getting to know us more, and inshallah they then get to learn about the more important things: our character and actions.

The Intellect needs a goal or purpose if it is to properly come into force. From something as simple as deciding what to eat, to the most complex task such as how to go about building an airport, the intellect is the servant of our goals.

The Intellect looks to solve problems and plan solutions; challenges come in all shapes and sizes. Some problems are posed by the Nafs: the intellect solves everyday things such as how to make food when you are hungry, or how to plan a safer route home if you are walking alone back from work at night.

The Intellect thrives best when it is set clear purposes and goals

If this is all you have though, then you might end up living your life pursuing only those things that are the products of desire: you miss out on the truer, deeper meaning of life. The Intellect truly thrives when we **keep it engaged, doing something that shows our value and fits our role.**

We do this by setting it to work achieving our aims, and by direct it towards things that bring us contentment. If you have a sufficiently engaged intellect, you will often find that your emotions are calm and under control, because the Nafs is also more calm and quiet when you are occupied in something industrious and productive. For many people, the highest meaning and contentment can be found when they find things that occupy their intellect in quiet productivity in this way.

As Muslims, we have an additional source of contentment: doing what Allah has asked us to do. If we use our intellect to make efforts learning about what makes for good conduct, helping our fellow human beings in the path to a respectful and dignified Islamic life, then we have surely discovered a great source of contentment.

Different people have different intellectual strengths. Where one person might be very good at building, another might be very good at organising events; yet another is a great designer, or cook, or great at teaching. There are different types of intelligence, and everyone should look to find where their strengths and enjoyment lies. Some people are blessed with very high intelligence in several areas, but this is not in itself a gift: a person must learn how to make the best use of their talents and find a way to make their skills match up to their roles and obligations.

The Intellect does not thrive on its own: it needs guidance as to what problems to solve, and what overall aims you have. Simply having a high intelligence is not a guarantee of good wisdom or good conduct: many highly intelligent minds have been deviated towards harmful thoughts and plans in pursuit of worldly desires and meaningless prizes.

Your true 'command station' should therefore be within your Heart. It is the place where you find the purposes and projects that you can set for your Intellect to then attend to. The Heart balances and guides both the Intellect and the Nafs. Once you have the purposes and goals in life decided by your Heart, the Intellect itself is given peace and purposeful activity.

In the battle that often occurs when the Intellect and the emotions are in conflict, siding with your Intellect is overall a better idea in most day to day situations, but be sure not to leave your Nafs out completely: your companionships, friendships, and your instincts about people are often better informed if you listen to your Nafs a little more, because your Nafs is more aware about sensing unwritten or unsaid things, such as telltale signs of imminent danger or trustworthiness in strangers.

The Intellect as we grow

As you grow, you can educate your Intellect with any amount of knowledge, expertise, and practice, creating and achieving things that you set out to do. Given the opportunities you have for education, be you fortunate to have access to the best, or if you only have meagre resources, the mission is the same: do your best with what you have, and find ways to interest and engage yourself with what Allah has put your way.

The way the Intellect works is interesting: it is in fact the harder or more challenging things that are likely to lead to growth, especially when you are an adult. The Intellect is best enabled when you face challenges with a sense of creativity and play: be optimistic and faithful that things will work out for the better, having the attitude that Allah will help you when your intentions and planning are good. This has a scientific basis too: people who learn a more positive mindset are significantly more creative and resilient.

Children have a very active and hungry Intellect, absorbing knowledge in their own way according to what kind of intellectual strengths they have. Some will love physical intelligence such as building, or athletic ability, or in interacting with others in play or trade. Others will enjoy and show skill in mathematics, others in art or history. It is important to help identify what they are good at and what they enjoy.

Alongside this, their Intellect thrives on having routine and structure. Introducing predictable schedules gives both us and our children a structure by which both they and we can foster growth. Alhamdulillah, the structure of salah times is also something that little children will readily adopt and follow if we demonstrate to them how it is just a part of our daily life: habits which are taught without fuss will become second nature, given time and explanation of benefit.

We all have different strengths and types of Intellect: some of us are strong in mathematics, others in the artistic, other in the physical intelligences like sports. It should be our duty, and joy, to identify our strengths and to use them to our best ability. Given time, the knowledge and skills we gather in the Intellect will help us to be very effective in our roles in life, and in acting towards the higher purposes and wisdoms that come from the Heart.

Types of Intellect

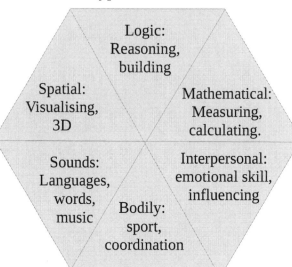

Logic: Reasoning, building

Spatial: Visualising, 3D

Mathematical: Measuring, calculating.

Sounds: Languages, words, music

Interpersonal: emotional skill, influencing

Bodily: sport, coordination

Choosing a career path

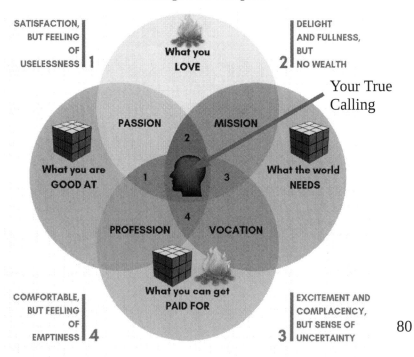

SATISFACTION, BUT FEELING OF USELESSNESS 1

DELIGHT AND FULLNESS, BUT 2 NO WEALTH

Your True Calling

What you LOVE

PASSION

MISSION

What you are GOOD AT

What the world NEEDS

PROFESSION

VOCATION

What you can get PAID FOR

COMFORTABLE, BUT FEELING OF EMPTINESS 4

EXCITEMENT AND COMPLACENCY, BUT SENSE OF 3 UNCERTAINTY

80

Think for yourself.
If you cannot, then you are a fool.
If you refuse to, you are a sinner.
If you dare not, you are a slave.

The Intellect is tranquil and focussed
When a person has decided on a steady purpose.

Being reasonable does not mean
Agreeing to everything.

Avoid argument when your anger is present.
Only then can your senses emerge.

Reasoning is when the emotions go to school.

A mind that is only logic, without wisdom,
Is like a knife without a handle.

If life throws you bricks and stones,
Use them to lay a foundation for yourself.

The final function of the Intellect is to realise
That there are things which are greater than it.

Take courage from remembering that
When your first efforts fail, the sky will not fall down.

INSTANT INSIGHTS

Chapter 5: The Heart: Your True Self

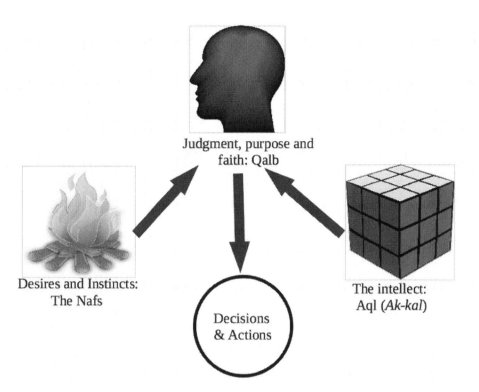

Judgment, purpose and faith: Qalb

Desires and Instincts: The Nafs

Decisions & Actions

The intellect: Aql (*Ak-kal*)

Alhamdulillah. The Heart is perhaps the greatest gift in the mind. In Arabic, the metaphorical word for Heart, when it comes to knowing your purpose and character, is Qalb.

You will find the Qalb mentioned many times in both Quran and Hadith. In essence, Allah has given us the Heart as the centre of our power to act out of free will. If anything symbolises the ability we have to understand ourselves, to have good conduct, and to make wise judgments in life, it is the Heart.

We have, with the Heart, the opportunity to use our morality, our judgment, and our common sense, to achieve the things we want to achieve, and to live in a way that brings us contentment, peace and benefits us and the people we love.

Left alone and untended, the Heart is weak and unable to control the Nafs and Intellect effectively. We have the responsibility, and the opportunity, to build the strength of character we need to be successful in whatever life throws at us. This is why Allah judges us based on what is within our Heart.

You, acting through your Heart, are the final judge and the examiner of your thoughts, feelings, actions and perceptions. Educating, informing, and looking after yourself is the route to all your aims and intentions in future.

Allah has connected your consciousness with your Nafs too: the mental consciousness is connected to the physical heart in your chest via the Nafs. When we are of settled mind, and clear conscience, the physical heart in your chest itself is healthy and calm: its rhythm is always closely connected to our mental state.

The Heart in this book is meant as the part of your mind where your true self is found. It can also be described as your Awareness: it is your concept of who you are, and your ability to decide your own aims and conduct. Your Heart can therefore be the supreme authority and force for good character in your life story.

The duties and functions of a strong Heart or Consciousness are as follows.

Listening to your mind

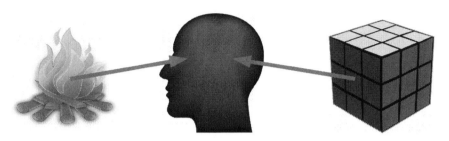

You Heart, or your Awareness, receives information from the Nafs and the Intellect. It is actually quicker to act than either: with a strong Heart, we can behave in a way that is sensible and automatic, avoiding the temptations and emotions of the Nafs and directing the Intellect towards good actions.

Inspecting what is going on in your mind

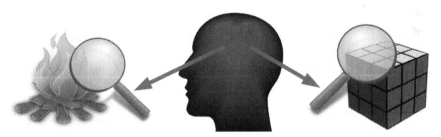

The Heart is like an Inner Eye with which you can look into yourself: you can use your Awareness to take note of what your thoughts or feelings are at any point. This neutral, non-judgmental self-observation is a very important tool for understanding how you are.

The more you do it, the better you will know yourself. We will talk more about this in the Chapter entitled 'Self Awareness'.

Weighing up the wisest way forward

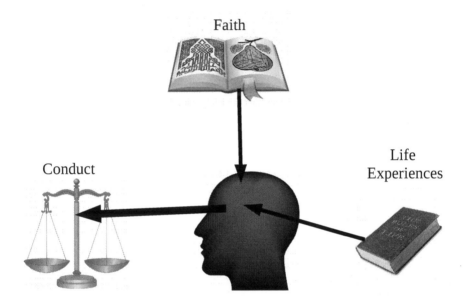

In matters where things are not clear, it is the Heart which has rules and laws which help us to make choices without having to re-examine them every time. This way, we save ourselves from looking to the Nafs or to the Intellect when we face some familiar, or difficult, issues and choices. It is a peaceful way of living, and the more we train the Heart, the better we get at it.

The Source of Wisdom and Purpose to Life

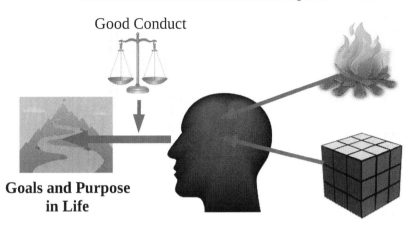

Good Conduct

**Goals and Purpose
in Life**

Finally and most importantly of all, we come to our reason for being. **The Heart is the seat of our faith, our purpose in life, and the place where we can define and refine our character.**

It is with your Heart that you find meaning and value in existence. Your Heart is the keeper and definer of your purpose and meaning in life.

Alhamdulillah, Allah has given us the freedom to choose what we want to believe in, and to choose our purposes in life. As Muslims, we have religious and material purposes and duties. We are here to do what Allah has asked us, and beyond this, we are to choose our other purposes and goals wisely. These are both explicitly religious things, and matters of *Akhlaaq* (good manners) that are of benefit and service to ourselves, our loved ones or indeed to the world as it is.

87

INSTANT INSIGHTS

Life shrinks or expands,
According to the size of your heart.

The windows of the masjid shine from within it is dark.
Your Heart should be like the masjid.

Carefully observe which way your Heart draws you,
Then follow that way with all your strength.

Throw your Heart into your beliefs
And the rest of you will follow.

However you treat yourself gives other people a guide
As to how they ought to treat you.

Everyone is a fool for a few minutes every day.
Wise people just know how to stay within that limit.

If your neighbour's grass looks greener,
Maybe he is just putting more Islam into his land.

Patience is your Heart's greatest companion.

Strengthen your heart by caring intensely
For a few right things, and letting the rest be.

Wisdom is like a wide old tree:
no one person can embrace all of it on their own.

INSTANT INSIGHTS

Chapter 6: Making peace with yourself

Islam as a word comes from three root meanings, *peace, acceptance* and *submission. Muslim* has the same roots, and literally means *someone who is peaceful through having accepted and submitted.*

Alhamdulillah! The very words themselves have profound meaning as far as the mind is concerned.

As human beings, we are instructed to find peace through accepting and submitting to:
a)   Allah's will: the way in which he has created us, and the world.
b) Allah's instructions: the ways in which he wishes us to conduct ourselves.

The clue to getting these things right is to make peace with ourselves. In reality, the main obstacle to our inner peace comes from the battle we have internally to control our free will and our actions in a way that best reflects how we truly would like to be.

The Nafs is also described as the ego, tempted as it is by emotions, desires and impulses, undoubtedly where shaitan invites us. Most of our mental suffering, and our unwanted behaviour, comes from having poor knowledge of ourselves and poor understanding of Nafs.

Having a peaceful life comes from making peace with ourselves. This comes from accepting the twists and turns of our emotions and impulses, and accepting both the pleasant and unpleasant emotions that we experience from the Nafs. It is active all the time, reacting (mostly over-reacting) to the world around us, or being simply irrational and randomly generating unwanted feelings. We cannot pick and choose which emotions we have: they are just there.

Steps to peace:
1. Accept and acknowledge. The first step to peace is to simply acknowledge- accept, and submit to the fact that emotions are going to be there, and we would be foolish to deny their existence.

2. Let strong emotions pass. Emotions stay much longer when we try to fight them or ignore them. We just need to feel them anyway, and listen to what they are saying to us with curiosity and patience, but we choose not to act on them immediately. Negative emotions and temptations diminish when we have heard them, and given them space. They are extreme, and designed to make us panic. If we just listen without acting, we can accept that whatever they are saying is very likely to be an exaggeration, if it is true at all (sometimes it is just purely irrational- see chapter 3).

3. Calm the Nafs. Just like any machine, the Nafs will be better when it is given some exercise and space to use up its excess energies.

Give your emotions their required free time in unacceptable way. As it is very invested with our physical bodies, we can access and calm the Nafs though doing things that put the body through positive stresses. Salah, exercise, and muraqabah (peaceful observation and reflection) are effective here: more on these later.

The emotions and drives that we have are neither good nor bad. The Nafs is simply there: it is universal. It is a part of both our physical and spiritual existence.

Fighting versus understanding

The journey of life involves navigating our way through against temptations and destructive instincts, sometimes called the Jihad-ul-Nafs.

Jihad really means struggle, not fight. A struggle means a **persistent application of effort**. Sure, you could fight your emotions, or ignore them completely, but they only get more tense if you continue down this route. It is probably better to find an easier way through them. It will still be a struggle, but you will be far wiser and less exhausted in both the short and long term if you understand yourself, and find a way to make peace with yourself. This is a key principle throughout this book.

If you try to just use mindless willpower to control yourself, it is both exhausting and doomed to fail.

Willpower is a misleading and weak thing. It is the belief that your wish to avoid some strong habit is greater than your instincts or drives to do it. Consider smoking, or gambling: people have willpower, but it fails them. This is because it is better to accept that the temptation is there, and to find ways of avoiding it rather than engaging with it. Remove that gambling app; avoid buying cigarettes, and take something that will quell your cravings. Accept that willpower is not helpful.

Better to understand and work with your Nafs than to beat it down. It takes a bit more effort, but your emotions will calm down and be easier to manage in the long term, once you gain knowledge on how to deal with them peacefully and insightfully.

It is better not to simply ignore the Nafs. You have to deal with it in some way or another.

Like the fire, the Nafs can be friend or foe. Just like fire, the Nafs can hurt us if we ignore it. The best way is to get to know how it works, which in turn gives us the opportunity to control it. Fires get hotter when we blow on them frantically trying to put them out. On the other hand, if we let a fire that is roaring just burn down on its own, while watching it from a safe distance, we see that it just calms down. It is as if the fire is tamed by our careful observation. And so it is with emotions.

The Nafs deals in *feelings and impressions.* So, we know the Nafs is active when we have a feeling- a strong emotion- about something.

How to deal with strong emotions, aka Nafs

Physical activity

Because Nafs is so much a part of your physical body, exercise is a great way of letting its excess energies just burn off. When we are tense, we notice how the whole body is affected: stiff muscles, sweating, nervous jitters, and what have you. This is a sign that the body needs to be exercised. When we do this, the result is that we release tension. Physical exercise has a natural way of calming the emotions. We end up feeling relaxed because we have given the body a physical workout, which is a great outlet for emotions that are otherwise pent up.

Deliberate exercise

The Nafs is more easily dealt with by physically tiring yourself out in a deliberate and methodical way.

It is astonishing how well an hour of exercise, or a long walk, or some vigorous pastime, even cleaning and tidying, will do to give the body, and therefore the Nafs, a sense of having achieved something fairly straightforward and concrete, and depleting excess free energy which would otherwise turn into burdensome tension or emotion.

Look at the animals: their entire lives are spent running, flying, swimming, escaping, searching. The Nafs is designed for a very physically active life. It is therefore crucial that we schedule exercise for ourselves at least 3 times a week. By this, I mean a period of around twenty minutes which sees us becoming breathless.

For some, this might be achieved through housework. For others, it is running, swimming, riding horses, or going to the gym. For those less able, even a walk for 20 minutes three times a week is a great method to settle the emotional body, releasing the energy and calming the Nafs down substantially.

<u>The physical benefits of Salah</u>

In a day's worth of salah, you will have accomplished:
- 50 minutes of standing on your feet.
- 48 flexions of the hips in ruku.
- 48 extensions of the back when rising back up.
- 48 squats of the thighs when standing up.
- 96 stretches of the arms in sijdah.
- More than an hour of quiet contemplation and focus.

When we are engaged in salah, from early morning, we are exercising the muscles of our entire body, and giving them a gentle stretch too. Doing salaah in a proper way is a great start to using the body, settling it down, aligning the muscles freshly each time, and wringing out the flesh. Standing, bending, squatting, getting up- all of this is a great boost to out physical body.

Question unwelcome feelings using your Intellect

The Intellect looks for truth and evidence. So, you can think of it like a detective, asking questions to seek truth and evidence, testing the Nafs' impulses for how accurate they are.

For example, you see someone who has a very nice house. You sense yourself becoming jealous. Jealousy is telling you that you deserve the same thing, and you get angry or sad that you don't have the same house. Your feelings convince you that you will not be happy until you have the same or better house. Your Intellect will look for evidence and facts behind the assumptions.

You could ask things as follows:

a) Is there evidence that having a nice house equals happiness? The logical answer is probably not. Many people with very nice houses are not happy. Happiness is not related to having nice houses.

b) Would you like a nice house anyway? Maybe. In that case, you should set out to save your money, or find good and honest ways of earning enough to get such a house. That way, you could satisfy the Nafs' aim to have security and status, without compromising on your morals or happiness.

The Nafs most frequently confuses **pleasure** with **long term contentment**. Logic will tell you that these are two different things. Having nice things is only really a short term pleasure: once you have them, the uncontrolled Nafs quickly finds another reason to be unhappy.

Use the wisdom of your Heart to comfort the Nafs

Listen to your Nafs sympathetically, and give yourself comfort and direction by offering a balanced and wise view.

Let's stick with the example of wanting the nice house. You feel this urge strongly; you see others with nice houses, and imagine what it would be like to live in such a place. This is most likely coming from the Nafs- it is the nesting instinct, perhaps along with the Nafs' love of status.

You can understand the desire for a nice house because your Nafs would want for you to feel safe, and secure, and to have respect and status in the community. These things are not wrong in themselves, but they can become excessive and dominate you.

Allah has made it halal for us to seek nice things, and in fact encourages us to wear nice clothes and have beauty in our life, as long as we do so without malice or deception, and that we keep in mind that we are doing so because it pleases Allah; it is not in an effort to make others jealous or to show off.

Possessions and luxuries are just part of a transient world, and having them has no bearing on a person's character, neither any bearing on the person's status in the eyes of Allah.

In essence, the Heart recognises the needs of the Nafs, and decides that some of it is useful: it would be a good thing to get a house. Once you have decided upon this firmly, a wise person would instruct their Intellect to take steps to work towards the house in a logical, planned, and sensible way, be it saving your money, finding extra work, or becoming better qualified to earn more.

Be thankful. Say Alhamdulillah!

Listening to your Heart will inform you that you can find happiness in every moment of your life.

Whatever things you possess, and whatever ultimately happens to you, is Allah's will. You are simply here to make efforts to use your mind and body as best you can. Achieving wisdom and good deeds may come or not: it doesn't matter, as long as your intentions are clear and sincere. You have no control over the consequences of your efforts in the world as such.

This should come as a great relief. It is an opportunity to thank Allah for everything you have, and to ask for what you want, knowing that the only reason you don't have it is because it is not part of your destiny right now. Your destiny is within your control if you are thankful and mindful of Allah, and make peace with your feelings and urges, accepting what you cannot change.

It should becomes clear what you have to do regardless of what happens in life: for everything that happens, or doesn't, praise

Allah. This is the best possible life for you, and part of His decisions for you which you must accept and be thankful for.

It is better to praise Allah for everything you have, rather than to be upset about what you don't. The gift of life, of food, water and family: all of those things are not guaranteed for anyone. If you have them, your emotions, if left unmonitored, will have you to take these blessings for granted. To counteract this problem, your Heart, being the seat of your faith, must remind you that all the things you have are merely temporary; their presence in your life is a constant gift from Allah.

Distract your Nafs

Dealing with the same problem: the wish to have nice things, can be difficult if you let it stew in your mind. If you leave it, it becomes bigger: soon, your Nafs will have you believe that it is the only thing that matters. You can prevent it from doing that by distracting yourself. So much of good mental health is based on occupation and distraction.

Doing something that is creative, or preoccupying, also has a great calming effect: Arts, Crafts, having a constructive hobby, and socialising and talking to other good people are all very good ways to distract the Nafs, and put your emotions back into a proper perspective. When you get to step away from a problem, it seems much less potent when you return to it.

Recognise that emotions are often just plain *irrational*

When you are sleepy, tired or otherwise not fully awake or otherwise weary, the Nafs can be particularly cheeky. You can become very quickly emotional, for no reason, over the smallest things. Things which didn't bother you suddenly seem very big.

You must know that your emotions are quite capable of being totally irrational: random, nonsense feelings and urges can come at any time, but especially when you are tired or drained. Seeing this for what it is- pure irrationality- can help you to just name it as an irrational feeling **that will pass**.

All feelings, especially irrational ones, will pass eventually. Name them as just passing feelings, and let them go of their own accord. Bearing this in mind will often help you to get through times when you simply don't understand them.

The basic summary of this chapter is that the emotions and instincts we have, as encapsulated in the concept of Nafs, are a permanent and powerful force in our lives. Neither good nor bad, we must understand them and learn how to use them for the better.

Emotion, inspiration and instinct are responsible for some of the best, and worst, qualities of humanity. They drive us to be inspired to achieve good things, yet they can also drive us to despair and lust after things which we do not actually need, and which don't really matter.

Your Intellect and your Heart are the keys to making sense of the messages the Nafs sends you. Sometimes your emotions will make no sense at all; you are still responsible for managing them, accepting that they are irrational and patiently seeing them out.

You are well advised to think of the Nafs as a very basic form of decision-making, suitable for animals but limited in its usefulness for human beings: we must therefore learn about it, and know how to accept and deal with its ups and downs.

Challenge negative thoughts directly

The table over the next two pages illustrates some typical negative thoughts that we all encounter in life, and also sets out some of the ways in which we can accept, challenge, accommodate and otherwise reduce their negative impact on us.

Remember, again, that the Nafs is neither good nor bad, but one thing remains true: whatever we face, the Nafs tends to make us overreact. Tending to it, understanding it and managing it properly, curbing its excesses while using it where it is useful, will help us to make peace with ourselves.

Problem and example	Origin	Emotional strategy: Acceptance	Intellectual Strategy: Seek out the truth	Strategy: Heart Use higher wisdom and faith
Mind Reading "So and so will say no when I ask him for something"	The Nafs prefers to stay cautious and protect itself from adventure or risk.	As above	I don't know what someone is thinking about. It is better to ask someone to see what they think. Do some research to find out how to be persuasive.	It is wiser to learn about people based on actual experience rather than your imagination. Use your intuition to read how ready people are to be asked. Accept whatever answer you get; at least you asked.
Fortune telling "I will never be happy"	As above. Plus the Nafs would rather you stayed unhappy because it protects from further disappointment.	As above.	I can't predict the future. There will be times when I am happy. People with less than I can be happy; my happiness will come.	Allah controls the future, not you. All misery will pass. Making the most of your life, good or bad, is the key to contentment. Practice gratitude and self awareness more.

Typical Negative Emotional Thoughts, and Strategies to Challenge them

Problem and example	Origin	Emotional strategy: Acceptance	Intellectual Strategy: Seek out the truth	Strategy: Qalb Use higher wisdom and faith
Black-or-white thinking "I am a failure"	The Nafs does not see complexity; it desires total victory	Accept all emotions as temporary and excessive. Patience	I have failed this time, but succeeded at many other things. I can learn where I went wrong and try again, better next time.	Failure is part of the route to success. Success or failure is Allah's will. Failure is an event, not a person.
Over-generalisation "I always get it wrong"	The Nafs exaggerates reality to the point where our estimations become extreme	As above	I've got things right many times before. I got it wrong this time. Doesn't mean I always get it wrong.	You win some, you lose some, despite your best effort. The wise person cares for humble effort and persistence.
Selective memory "I've never been happy"	The Nafs dominates what we remember depending on what mood we are in at the time.	As above	I have been happy; it is harder to remember those times when I am sad.	Practice gratitude for the small blessings you have every day. This will grow to great contentment over time.

105

REFLECTIONS

You are not on a cruise ship. You are on a lifeboat.
The trick is to try to be cheerful even if you feel lost.

Few things are ever as urgent
As your stress would imply.

Make time to relax,
Or else you won't have time to work.

Prefer to eat a crumb in peace
Than a whole cake in anxiety.

True wealth is not from having more possessions.
It is from wanting less.

If you begin to believe your work is too important,
You are heading for a nervous crash.

If you are chasing something around the earth,
Slow down. It will come round and catch you.

Be reassured, it is difficult to find peace:
It is harder, in fact, than engaging in battle.

Peace is not the absence of conflict:
It is the ability to deal with conflict peacefully.

INSTANT INSIGHTS

Chapter 7: Dealing with Negative Emotions: RIADH, The Garden of Instant Peace.

Negative emotions are a part of normal life. It would be useful to know how to deal with them if they are there right now. This chapter gives you a powerful method.

The first thing to know is that we over-react to everything. This is part of our design- Alhamdulillah! We learn that emotions are part of our *insaaniyat* (our humanity), and that most emotions arise from our Nafs- the more primitive, basic side of our human mind and body.

Emotions are mostly tied to things that the Nafs is concerned with: survival, conflict, pride, jealousy, fear and so on. The problem is that even though we are in the modern world, emotions have not caught up with wisdom: emotionally, the Nafs behaves as if it is part of the wild animal world. This is very wise of Allah; living in the modern world requires us to be aware that despite our modern advancements and comforts, we are still as a species inclined to behave in a selfish and destructive way; the Nafs is both a cause of that, and a method of understanding it so that we can protect and look after ourselves.

Alhamdulillah, if we think deeply, we recognise that negative emotions are signals telling us that the Nafs is not happy. The Nafs is concerned with the idea that we are facing some threat to our survival, rank, or status. Bear in mind though, we over-react: to everything. The truth is, therefore, emotions are almost always based on believing an exaggerated version of reality, or not on reality at all! When emotions set in, we are persuaded that something is much worse than it really is.

Emotions serve to amplify something, to make it seem bigger and scarier than it actually is. This happens because the Nafs is trying to get us to act. Remember though that the Nafs relies on feelings and impressions, not on facts and evidence.

Therefore we face a danger: we will react excessively, to something that isn't actually as bad as our Nafs would have us believe, or maybe it isn't actually there at all.

So, the emotions must be dealt with. In the chapter 6, 'Making peace with ourselves', we looked at different ways in which we can understand and manage the Nafs. Various ways and means exist, by which we can calm, challenge, distract or otherwise channel our desires and emotions so that either they are put to good use, or diminished in their intensity. But sometimes emotions can become very strong, and we need to learn about challenging them directly, in the moment, in real-time so to speak.

The RI'ADH method. Ri'adh means 'garden' in Arabic. Islamic Gardens are in 4 sections, with a pool of water in the middle. Imagine that your mind is a beautiful Islamic garden. It needs rain and sunshine, but not too much of either.

Now imagine emotions to be a storm cloud. The cloud is approaching your garden at great speed. How do you prepare for such an amount of rain all at once?

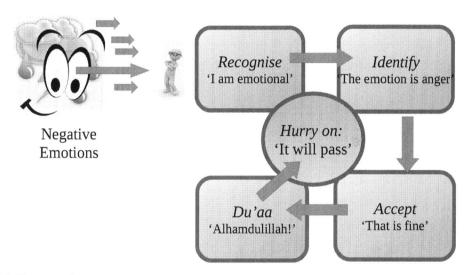

Negative
Emotions

Recognise
'I am emotional'

Identify
The emotion is anger'

Hurry on:
'It will pass'

Du'aa
'Alhamdulillah!'

Accept
'That is fine'

a) **Recognise**
Recognise that you are being visited by emotion. Whatever the emotion, if it is strong then you need to give it the attention that it demands.

b) **Identify**
In the second garden, you identify the emotion: just <u>name</u> it. Clouds are of different types, just like emotions. Name it. Say to yourself: 'this is anger', or 'this is anxiety'.

c) **Accept**
The third garden is the garden of acceptance. Even unpleasant emotions must be accepted. n other words, **make peace with what is within you, even if it is unpleasant.**

You don't need to know why the emotion is there. You must simply just accept it. It is in your garden, and it is part of you. Do the cloud a great favour: don't fight it off. It is simply bringing rain. You are trying to be a peaceful and reasonable person, but to do so means you accept the parts of you that are unreasonable. This way, they don't have a hold of you. Every garden needs rain: sometimes rain comes in a storm. Just hold fast and it passes.

d) **Du'aa**
Say Alhamdulillah!
Thank Allah for your emotions, use them if they are useful, but just let them pass if they are not. Storm-clouds can have good or bad effects, just like your Nafs: it depends how you are prepared to accept them. The more you welcome it, the better you will get at dealing with it. Be patient with yourself: be thankful that you are designed in a way that is perfect in the way Allah intended.

e) **Hurry on.**
At the centre of the garden is a pool: this is where the rain can fall and drain away. Move on. Get on with what you were doing before the emotion came to disturb you.

A good host allows his guests to stay, even if they are unwelcome or irritating. If you keep arguing with guests, they will only just stay longer. In the same way, if you go out and start to fight with the rain and wind, or worse still, panic and behave like a cloud yourself, it is a pointless exercise. You will just end up damaging your garden.

So much unnecessary human mental suffering comes from a sense of being oppressed by our own emotions. When we simply accept the emotions, we are showing something called **meta-cognition**- thinking about our own minds- which in turn makes us far more powerful over ourselves. We get to see the Nafs for what it is: just a signalling system that we could respond to *in any way that we like. We recognise that we have a choice.*

Mental illness

All negative emotions are temporary, and they will all get bored, tired and drained, and leave us if we let them just be. If they do not, for example if they linger and are inconsolable, or if our thoughts become detached from reality, impacting our functioning, then we must consider if we are becoming mentally ill: if this occurs, advice and consultation from a doctor or similar professional must be sought. If you spot this in someone else, help them. Allah commands us to look after ourselves when we are ill, in body or in mind.

Clinical depression is when a person is convinced of hopelessness; nothing convinces them otherwise, and it is impossible to cheer up beyond a few minutes. The person seems to have lost all perspective on their problems, for weeks on end.

Paranoid illness happens when a person believes their life is being sabotaged in some sinister way. It typically happens after some negative event, and can be accompanied by hearing voices or other strange phenomena. People with this need us to recognise it and get them professional medical help.

REFLECTIONS

When a storm arrives, just keep sailing.

There is a deep and wise beauty that arrives
From being broken and repaired again and again.

Do not begrudge crying.
Tears wash the eyes, giving you a better focus.

If you let your fear outgrow your faith,
Your hopes and dreams diminish.

Old Man Panic casts a much longer shadow
Than his actual size.

Fearing pain is the same as suffering from fear.

Maybe the glass is neither half full nor half empty;
Maybe you have enough water, and a big glass.

Your grey matter is grey for a reason:
The world is not black or white.

Moments of stress are moments of time
Just before you realise it doesn't really matter.

God doesn't give you things
As much as he puts you near things you could use.

INSTANT INSIGHTS

Chapter 8: Guidance from your Heart

The Heart, also known as your conscious awareness and free will, is the keeper and definer of our purposes and missions in life. The Heart is what we are judged on. It is the true self, because it is accountable and conscious of what we do. It therefore has responsibility for managing our thoughts, feelings and actions in the course of life.

To achieve our purposes in life, the Heart could be said to be underpinned by the Laws of Deen: guidance about the nature of humanity, and facts which guide us forward in dealing with life as it really is. These could be called the **Rules of Conduct** and the **Truths of Life**.

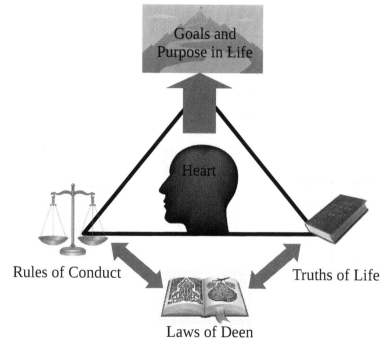

Alhamdulillah: in reality, our Deen, from the Quran and Hadith, contains a comprehensive guidance in all elements of wisdom: religious rules, good conduct, and the truths of the material world. It is only for the sake of understanding that I have separated the elements so that we can examine them more closely.

Our aim in life is to conduct ourselves in a way that is wise and successful, both in Deen (religion) and in Dunya (the material world). The Laws of Deen are immutable: they include, principally, our obligations in terms of the five pillars of Islam. Alhamdulillah, there are many books with great guidance and instruction on how we can strive towards fulfilling these aims, and more beyond.

The Truths of Life, and the Rules of Conduct are part of our beliefs and our manners: overall, called *Akhlaaq (overall character)*. Having good our Akhlaaq is relevant to managing our minds in a correct and effective way in an everyday sense. Getting these things right will help us to navigate everyday life in a far easier way.

Our purpose

Your Heart is like a mission control centre. Within the Heart we can define your purposes, which can be broadly categorised into two areas: religious obligations, and material aims.

118

The importance of the Heart in defining everything we do

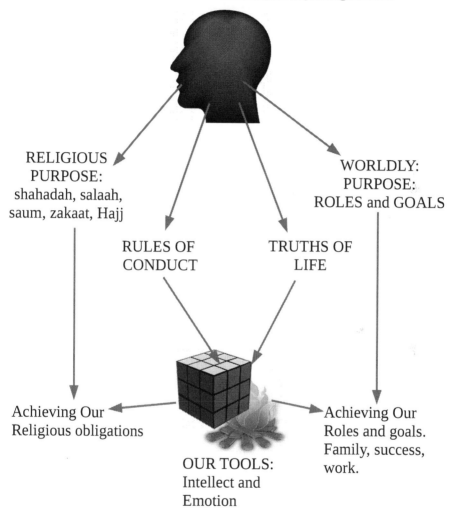

RELIGIOUS
PURPOSE:
shahadah, salaah,
saum, zakaat, Hajj

WORLDLY:
PURPOSE:
ROLES and GOALS

RULES OF
CONDUCT

TRUTHS OF
LIFE

Achieving Our
Religious obligations

Achieving Our
Roles and goals.
Family, success,
work.

OUR TOOLS:
Intellect and
Emotion

The Heart is the source of **why we are here**. As we can see, it is the Heart that keeps us true to our aims and purposes in life.

The Intellect deals with the **what** and the **how**: knowing the rules, setting the goals, and setting out how to achieve them step by step.

The Nafs gives us a sense of **energy** and **motivation**. Using it properly helps propel us along, even guiding us to watch out for threats and dangers when we are properly tuned into it.

A strong Heart keeps us focussed on what is important, instructs and manages the Intellect and Nafs, and thereby guides us as to how to behave and manage ourselves, and ensures that we conduct ourselves in a way that is both productive and wise.

Without the Heart we are directionless and lacking in good Akhlaaq (conduct). We would find life without meaning, and both the Intellect and Nafs would find themselves trying to muddle through things without a sense of *why.*

The Truths of Life

These are facts which will help us to stay grounded and real.

Life is full of good and bad experiences. We learn from them as we go along. However, we don't all learn at the same rate: some of us keep making the same mistakes, apparently unaware of why some things keep going wrong for us. We can and will learn from some mistakes, but we won't learn from others. The Truths of Life are facts which keep us oriented to reality. They are very useful in guiding our decisions as to what we will do, and managing our reactions to whatever happens to us.

We are well advised to keep these Truths of life close to our consciousness.

Here are some examples of Truths of Life:

- Life on earth seems unfair. We must accept this without becoming upset every time. We must acknowledge reality and move forward.
- The present moment is the only time we have control over. The past and the future are not here.
- Everything in life is temporary: good times, and bad times, don't last forever.
- Expectations in life are always changing. People change the goalposts without our knowing it. We must adapt, not get infuriated.
- People lie, and deceive, and people act selfishly. We might spot this sometimes, or we might not.
- We cannot get along with everyone. We will be disappointed, and we will disappoint others.
- Bad things happen to good people, and good things happen to bad people. We cannot see Allah's reasons.
- Not everything works out. Our prayers will seem unanswered; we must accept this with a steady hand and a thankful heart, and make our efforts nonetheless.
- We make our efforts to do whatever we do, but the results of our efforts are at the mercy of Allah. We may not understand the results, or why things happen.
- Life turns out better for those who deal with ups and downs as they are, not as they expect them to be.

These truths are the kinds of things which we are taught, or what we learn by our own experiences. Knowing them, and reminding yourself of them often, will be a great tonic and refresher when you feel maddened or weary about bad times, and conversely, when you get too elated in the good times. Moderation comes from understanding the truth.

We get the Truths wrong when we confuse them with **expectations and beliefs.** When our expectations or beliefs are incorrect, we will keep arriving at the wrong conclusion about something, and this grinds us down to a state of despair and confusion. Some examples of erroneous expectations and beliefs which are erroneous are outlined in the table at the end of chapter 6.

Reflecting on ourselves (see chapter 9), and seeking guidance from Allah, will give us a steady stream of Truths of Life which are a tremendous blessing from Allah: they will assuage our pain, and steady our minds, through thick and thin. Life has its ups and downs, but the Truths of Life remain the same.

The Rules of Conduct

Rules of Conduct are goals of **how you would like to behave**. These too are outlined in Islamic teachings and taught to us by teachers and parents. It is important, and very helpful indeed, that you declare what your most important Rules of Conduct are, and just like the Truths of Life, you should remind yourself of them frequently: some choose to have them written down somewhere readily visible to them, and even look them over every day.

Think about your character as a lump of coal. Coal is made of carbon: the same element that all living things are made of. Now, depending on what you do to carbon, it can end up in a number of different states:

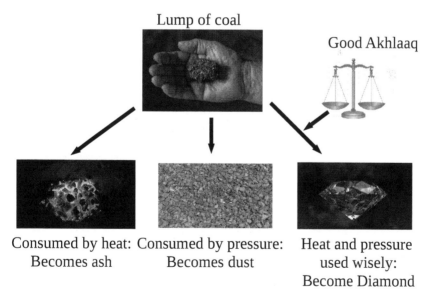

Lump of coal

Good Akhlaaq

Consumed by heat: Becomes ash

Consumed by pressure: Becomes dust

Heat and pressure used wisely: Become Diamond

Life will grind you down, burn you, or polish you up:

It depends how you handle it. The lump of coal can be turned into ash, coal dust, or diamond, all through the same processes: heat and pressure. The fate of the lump of coal depends on how it reacted to its particular circumstances.

Your character is a bit like that lump of coal. It will go through many tests. It will face pressure, temptations, and dilemmas. If you have nurtured your wisdom with good Akhlaaq, you will not only find pressure and difficulty easier to handle, but you can also use those same forces to achieve happiness and success. Life will grind you down, or polish you up: it depends how you handle it.

Devising your Rules of Conduct:
'I will try to be...'

We have morals and laws which our Deen teaches us. Those are givens. Honesty, compassion, and so on. But we must reflect on them, and continually hold ourselves to account as to how we are actually living those values out. Only if we really reflect on these things, every day, can we make them big and present in our minds and only then will they become set into our character.

If you were to keep your own Rules of Conduct close to you, even written down, somewhere you can see them every day, then it is easier for you to remember to look at them, and think about them, for at least a few minutes, every day.

This takes effort, but you can easily add it in to your time before or after salaah, or to those few moments you take for yourself when having coffee, breakfast or going to work.

To devise your own personal Rules, try these exercises:

1. Cast your mind forward in time. Imagine yourself very old, and looking back on your life. You will be facing Allah. When you face Allah, what character would you be proud of having shown throughout your life?

2. Imagine yourself giving advice to a much younger version of you; maybe you were just a young child. Imagine you were writing down a set of 20 rules that the child had to read, every morning and night. They had to act out those rules every day in order become a good and worthy person. What would those rules be?

3. Think of some words that describe the kind of qualities you would like to show, every day.

Over the page are some examples.

Here are some examples of the Rules of Conduct.

"I will try to be..

- **Thankful.** To thank Allah for what I have, and always remember what others less fortunate me do not have, or have lost.
- **Hopeful.** To retain hope, for myself and for other people. Hope is what gets me through difficulty, and conquers fear.
- **Purposeful.** To involve myself in something that is important and that matters to me and the people I love.
- **Loving.** To show and demonstrate my love for the people whom I love, in a concrete and regular way.
- **Committed.** To do what I am obliged to do, and what I have planned to do, humbly and without emotional interference, without waiting for my mood or motivation to be right.
- **Cheerful.** To smile every morning, and remember to approach every new thing with a positive attitude.
- **Individual.** To pursue and develop my own particular strengths, to value myself and be of use to other people.
- **Accountable.** To take responsibility for my decisions even when things turn out badly.
- **Loyal.** Family is more important than work.
- **Dignified.** To act in a manner that shows gentleness, humility and quiet strength.

The Rules of Conduct are especially helpful when you are in the midst of an emotional storm and can't easily think of sensible or logical ways forward because your Nafs is dominating your thinking. The Rules also help you to take more responsibility for your actions and choices, giving you greater control over your destiny.

Rules of Conduct are part of the higher mission of why you exist, with a meaning and purpose beyond just surviving, even beyond just living harmoniously with others. You should pay close attention to your Rules of Conduct. People don't often think about them as much as they should.

Keep them close, written down, revise them, draw them out from when you learn about Deen, and take time to repeat them frequently; some people do this every day, others only periodically. Do what you need to do; the more you put in, the more you gain. Inshallah, you will strengthen your Heart, and these truths will be written in your heart, and guide your every action from the moment you wake.

Rules of Conduct are what I like to think of as a set of golden rules and instructions, defined by you, as to what beliefs you hold dear, and how you conduct yourself. They are designed to give you, above everything else, greater insight into how you can take responsibility for your choices and actions. The greater your understanding your role in how things turn out for you, and the higher the quality of your Rules of Conduct, the greater your control over your destiny. Allah has given us many rules of conduct. We must focus on them, and be mindful of reminding ourselves of them every day.

Rules of Conduct as described in the Quran

The Quran and Hadith have set down many thousands of rules and laws as to how we should conduct ourselves. This whole area, known as the Shariah, is complex and comprehensive. However, to keep things simple and to give the reader of an idea of the kind of rules that we come across, here are just some of the rules that are spelled out in the Quran. We would be well advised to read and re-read them with deep reflection and thought, as frequently as time will allow. Inshallah they will help us to conduct ourselves in a way that earns Allah's blessing and keeps us happy and content.

Don't lie (22:30)
Don't spy (49:12)
Don't insult (49:11)
Don't waste (17:26)
Feed the poor (22:36)
Don't backbite (49:12)
Keep your oaths (5:89)
Don't take bribes (27:36)
Honour your treaties (9:4)
Restrain your anger (3:134)
Don't spread gossip (24:15)
Think good of others (24:12)
Be good to guests (51:24-27)
Don't harm believers (33:58)
Don't be rude to parents (17:23)
Turn away from ill speech (23:3)
Don't make fun of others (49:11)
Walk in a humble manner (25:63)
Respond to evil with good (41:34)
Don't say what you don't do (62:2)
Keep your trusts & promises (23:8)
Don't insult others' gods (6:108)

Don't deceive people in trade (6:152)
Don't take items without right (3:162)
Don't ask unnecessary questions (5:101)
Don't be miserly nor extravagant (25:67)
Don't call others with bad names (49:11)
Don't claim yourselves to be pure (53:32)
Speak nicely, even to the ignorant (25:63)
Don't ask for repayment for favours (76:9)
Make room for others at gatherings (58:11)
If enemy wants peace, then accept it (8:61)
Return a greeting in a better manner (4:86)
Don't remind others of your favours (2:264)
Make peace between fighting groups (49:9)
Lower your voice and talk moderately (31:19)
Don't let hatred cause you to be unjust (6:108)
Don't ask too many favours from people (2:273)
Greet people when entering their home (24:27)
Don't be too expressive in your jubilation (28:76)
Be just, even against yourself & relatives (4:135)
Speak gently, even to leaders of disbelief (20:44)
Don't criticize small contributions of others (9:79)
Don't call the Prophet how you call others (24:63)
Try to make peace between husband & wife (4:128)
Oppression/corruption is worse than killing (2:217)
Preach to others in a good and wise manner (16:125)
Don't accuse others of immorality without proof (24:4)
Consider wives of the Prophet like your mothers (33:6)
Don't call someone a disbeliever without knowing (4:94)
Seek permission before entering someone's room (24:59)
Know your enemies can become your close friends (41:34)
Don't wrongly consume the wealth of the vulnerable (4:29)
Don't turn your cheek away from people in arrogance (31:18)
Forgive others, as you would like Allah to forgive you (24:22)
Don't hold secret meetings for sin, rather do so for piety (58:9)
Don't order others to do good while forgetting it yourself (2:44)
Be patient with your teacher & follow his instructions (18:67-69)

Don't frown, turn away or neglect those who come to you (80:10)
If unable to help a needy person, at least speak nice words (17:28)
Be lenient to those under you, and consult them in matters (3:159)
Verify information from a dubious source before acting upon it (49:6)
Those who can should continue to spend on those less fortunate (24:22)
Don't enter homes without permission & return if refused entry (24:27-28)
Don't sit with those who mock religion until they change the subject (4:140)
Say it's not appropriate to talk of slander when it's mentioned to you (24:16)
Divorce in an amicable manner instead of keeping & harming your wife (2:231)
Punish in an equivalent manner to how you were harmed, or be patient (16:126)
Differences in colour & language are signs of Allah, not means of superiority (49:13)
Don't take women by force, nor take back bridal gift without a valid reason & live with them in kindness (4:19)

Great minds have roles and purpose.
Lesser minds have demands and wishes.

If Allah has made you,
Then he has surely found a use for you.

Accept reality, but also persist
In making reality accept your purpose.

Guard your integrity:
Lies might get you ahead, but you can never go back.

He who is rude is somewhat in the wrong,
Regardless of how truly he speaks.

You could rob your character to enrich your pocket,
But your character is harder to recover than wealth.

How someone treats you is their path to travel;
How you react is yours.

Laws control the lesser man.
Good conduct controls the greater one.

Dignity comes from behaving in a prizeworthy way;
Never from seeking the prize itself.

INSTANT INSIGHTS

Chapter 9: Self Awareness and Reflection

You will remember from Chapter 5 that one of the functions of the Heart- the true self- is to pay attention to things. It is like the mind's eye, which you can use to observe, investigate and reflect on how you are:

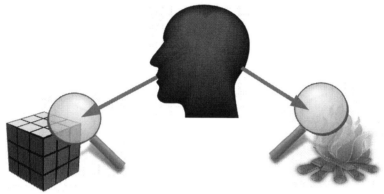

Self awareness is how much we know about our own character and ability. How much do you truly know about yourself, in different circumstances? How are you when you are happy, sad, giddy, stressed, lost, alone? Primarily, you gain knowledge about yourself by reflecting on your thoughts and actions. How much did your actions reflect your best behaviour? How much did your actions reflect you were acting with good *Akhlaaq* (manners)?

When we go through life, we experience it in many senses: we hear, see, feel, touch, remember, perceive, and emote. All of this requires all parts of our mind to be in sync. How do we give this process a break? How do we let it calm down, so we can see how we are doing, and where it needs help? The answer lies in how much we practise reflection.

True self awareness comes when we reflect on ourselves, deeply and frequently. Ideally, we should undertake reflection several times a week, taking time especially in Fajr time or after Esha at night. We could think about our self awareness in the following way:

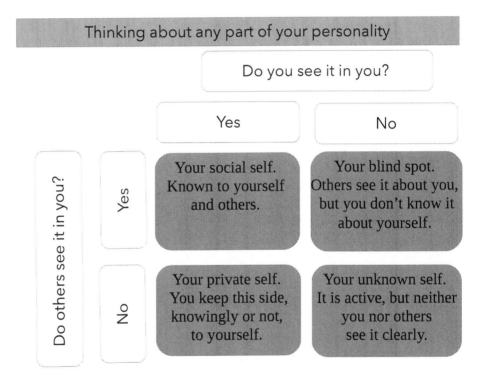

Alhamdulillah. We are complex people who don't know ourselves entirely, and we constantly have to keep attending to our self awareness as time goes by: we evolve different view about ourselves and other people as we grow older, we show different parts of ourselves in different situations, and we change our beliefs and attitudes to things as we go through life.

134

In learning about who we are, we must take the time to reflect upon our actions, daily. Thoughts become actions, actions become habits, and habits become character.

Reflection upon yourself is a simple process, but simple things are often overlooked because they seem almost too straightforward for the rewards they could bring. In essence, reflection is when you observe yourself calmly and without judgment, using the Heart as an inner eye. The process is deeply calming and very illuminating. You gain a sense of calmness by observing the Nafs and the Intellect for what they are, and you give them a voice and chance to be understood which is much deeper than just the everyday sense of a simple story.

A framework for reflection

Reflection is a process of active remembering your ABCs: Antecedents, Behaviours, Consequences. In other words, we can look at events in our life by asking:

Antecedents: what happened leading up to the behaviour? What mood or state of mind was I/ someone else in? How did I/ they perceive things?

Behaviour: How did I/ they react? What led to my decision to act in the way I did?

Consequences: What was the result? Did things work out well? Was it a win-win or did someone lose out in some way?

Taking time to reflect on your actions, on any given day, increases your ability to understand your role in what happens in your life. With anything that happens, we can see the ABC. The event, the actions that took place, and the consequences of that action.

For any events that happen in any one day, thinking through the ABCs gives you an insight into what you did, in a time and space that allows you to see yourself a little bit from the outside.

An example of simple reflection

Supposing you went and bought a book today. So, nothing much to think about on the surface. But supposing you regretted buying that particular book, and when you get home you notice that you have a collection of books which you frequently regret buying.

When you reflect on it, you will discover the way in which your attention was caught when you needed to learn something, and how you resolved to find a book which would explain it. You will remember how the need came from a sense of seeming ignorant about the subject when you saw a piece about it on TV. You will remember browsing around the different books online, getting lost in other lurid subject titles, and then deciding to go with one which had the best reviews over the one which seemed the more colourful.

In this way, reflection helps you to gain an insight into your decisions and motives. You learn that you were more motivated by conforming to others' views than by what made you happy. This is something you can become more aware of next time round. This, then, is the power and beauty of reflection. Reflection is one of the finest and most powerful things that you can do to gain mastery over yourself. It is therefore VERY important that we make time to reflect on ourselves.

Example two

Supposing you met someone just for a chat, and things didn't go well. You didn't see eye to eye with them and you left each other a little disappointed. Looking back at it, what did you hear them say, and what was your reaction? Were you being quick to judge them? Did you quite hear what they were trying to say? If they were upset, did you do anything to make that happen? What could you have done to make things go better next time?

The point of reflection is to observe yourself: your actions and reactions, not theirs. You need only be curious, not judgmental. You only need to ask the question: what was I like? No need to be interested in judging yourself positively or negatively. You are just learning about how you acted, what character you showed, and in this, you will learn how much you are driven by your Nafs, or by your Intellect.

So really, reflection is a bit like being an editor of your own life movie. Imagine you are no longer acting the scene: it is recorded, and now you are in the editing room. Playing it back, what do you observe about yourself? What can you learn about the feelings and actions you took at the time?

Even if you don't know how to change your actions for the better next time, you still have made an important step: you are more aware of who you are, and by playing your life back to yourself, have a better awareness and memory of your character.

Evidence suggests that people who do take time out to reflect, even after a short period of 30 days, show clear changes in the way the brain operates: it is more settled, more at peace, and more rapid in its decision making. It stands to reason: the more you know yourself, the less effort and confusion you feel, and the quicker you can make decisions.

The Heart is best when we remember the instructions from Allah, and when we try our best to match up to the rules of conduct that we have set for ourselves. Reflect regularly, and frequently: a strong Heart needs repetition, attention, and constant minor revision.

In our journey to become at peace with ourselves and more spiritually connected to Allah, we are commanded by Him to become more insightful, to become more understanding of who we are.

<u>Methods that assist us in Reflection</u>

Du'aa (praying)   Journalling   Talking to a close
                                              person

138

Methods that assist us in reflection

1. Du'aa

In the evening du'aa, perhaps after Esha, or as you are turning into bed, do the following:

a) Think over the significant events in your day, think about and tell Allah about what happened to you, how you reacted, and what you did. He will listen intently to you. It is just you and Him.

b) If you are happy with how you thought and acted, tell him. If you are unhappy about it, tell him too. Reflect with sincerity on how you could change the way you act for the better, even in a slight way.

c) Tell Allah about what is coming up for you tomorrow, and how you hope to handle it. Ask him for your help in handling both expected and unexpected things in a good way, and promise Him that you will talk to Him again about your day tomorrow.

Alhamdulillah! We have the opportunity to pray to Allah at any time of day. We can do it within our own minds as we go about our day, or more formally around salah times.

Prayer is very much encouraged and welcomed by Allah, unconditionally. By encouraging us to make Du'aa, Allah has given us an excellent way of reflecting on ourselves.

Du'aa is a guaranteed method of reflection that will have you become much more self aware. If you do it every day, within 30 days of doing it, inshallah you will definitely become a lot more insightful and self aware.

When we make reflective du'aas in this way, we give voice to our feelings, our regrets, and our intentions, telling Allah about them. We make ourselves humble students of our lives, and we ask Allah to help us to learn about who we are and how best to be good people.

2. Reflection using the diary/journal method

Some people like to write things down. A couple of lines in a diary is all it really takes, if that is what works. Or a voice memo on your phone. Saying things out loud, or recording them in writing, is clever because it causes you to put in words the feelings and urges that otherwise don't become concrete.

Emotional information doesn't easily find language: turning it into language by forcing yourself to write it down or say it to yourself, is one good way of ensuring it enters your Intellect, and your Heart, so that you can look at it more sensibly, and you can learn from it and apply wisdom to it.

Note: be careful to make sure that wherever you make such notes is private, for your eyes only. These days, anything we say and write can be misinterpreted and misused against us.

Example of a written reflection

Met J today. He seemed annoyed about the noise coming from my room. I had no idea it was that noisy- I told him that but he didn't believe me. I got annoyed at him because he didn't believe me. Maybe he was right. Maybe I was too noisy. He could have been less antsy about it though. Doesn't matter. Maybe I'll go round, and tell him I was sorry for the noise. And lower the volume a little. I hope Allah is pleased with this course of action.

3. Reflection by talking through with another person

For dilemmas that we are not sure about, we have the option of talking the matter through with someone else. Reflection with other people is especially helpful because they really can give us a more independent view. There are some things that you just can't see about yourself- your blind spots- which other people can. Talking something through can help you work out where your blind spots are, allowing you to understand yourself better and giving you yet more options about how to do things differently next time.

Choose very carefully who you reflect on personal things with. Ideally, they should have some sort of personal investment in you- that is, your happiness must impact upon them in some close and pertinent way. For personal things, in your private life away from work, this could be someone from your personal circle- someone with whom you have a degree of closeness with, such as a lifelong close friend or your spouse. Bonds of blood (i.e. family) are the strongest. Too often we forget how much of a help our grandparents, siblings, parents, or aunts and uncles can be just the right sounding board for our reflections provided we believe they are the right person to confide in.

Alternately, some people find it easier to confide anonymously to someone who is not connected to their life in any way. The modern world has helplines, counsellors, and various other agencies that might be os use. The important thing is not to confide in your acquaintance or work circle if you can possibly avoid it; such people are not in a position to truly have your best personal interests at heart, and they may find themselves conflicted or uneasy about hearing personal issues.

<u>Allah illuminates us the closer we get to His light.</u>

Remember that as Muslims we have the greatest of all companions- Allah himself. If you are alone, remember that things are exactly as they were written to be: you are never truly alone, because when there is no other person around, Allah has sent them away so that it can be just you and Him together. You are never truly alone. Allah himself is by your side when you humbly and earnestly make efforts to understand and improve yourself on your own.

Being consciously attentive is about knowing, first and foremost, that we have **choices** about how to interpret the things going on in our life, and choices as to how we react and conduct ourselves.

A side note: reflecting, not ruminating

Reflecting is, in essence, an active process where we gain self awareness. Reflecting is not to be confused with *ruminating*.

Ruminating is getting emotionally or mentally bogged down in the same problem without escape or relief; it is mostly involuntary, in that it happens outside your control and is difficult to stop. It is when your Intellect or your Nafs are preoccupied with something to the point where no solution is being sought or found, and the facts are distorted or exaggerated to the point where the issue seems much bigger than it really is. The issue just goes round and round, taking your mind out of the present moment and into some unchangeable issue from the past, or uncontrolled anxiety about the future.

Rumination happens when you lose the ability to supervise yourself, and become beholden to a troublesome and often exhausting mental trap. Ruminating can be prevented if you reflect on your life every day, for just a few minutes. Ruminations can get out of control if we are mentally ill. If you find yourself ruminating incessantly to the point where it is taking over your mind and impacting your day negatively, you are well advised to seek help from a professional: a doctor or counsellor can help to diagnose and treat the issue. Never suffer alone.

In regularly reflecting on the values you live by,
You become closer to the person you aspire to be.

When you recognise yourself fully,
Notice that you no longer remain what you once were.

Of all the mines of treasure,
The best gold is to be found within ourselves.

When you speak to Allah, you also hear yourself.
Listen to what you hear.

When you make du'aa, take time be silent afterwards.
Allah's answers will often be heard in that silence.

Reflection creates a space within you that allows
Your calmer character to come out and be seen.

Never make the mistake of thinking that when
People contradict you, you are not to be believed in.

Proper reflection finds you truths that need to be said,
And truths you never thought you could know.

A true friend is someone who knows you're a good egg
Even when you feel scrambled.

INSTANT INSIGHTS

Chapter 10: Attentiveness

"One hour's meditation on the work of the creator is better than seventy years of prayer"- Prophet Muhammad SAW

Attentiveness is when you are focussed. It is when your Heart is in charge of your mind. It makes life a lot easier. Many of the everyday decisions we face can be dealt with by the Heart effortlessly. A truly attentive person finds it easy to define what they want to do, and to go about doing it. The attentive Heart does two things:

a) reminding you of how you wish to conduct yourself, and of the purposes and roles that you need to attend to.

b) observing and marshalling your Nafs and Intellect in a way that keeps them on side, calm and productive.

All parts of the mind pay attention, but they do so differently.

- The Nafs is scattered in its attention, flitting between the past, present and future rapidly, getting confused and alarmed about things if we let it. Emotional memories are biased, and grainy, prone to errors and revisions without our knowing.

- The Intellect prefers to look at the present and the future, focussed on solving the many everyday problems and things that need to be done. Your intellect enjoys being given a goal but is blind to higher purposes.

- The Heart is your main tool of attention to observe yourself in a more objective, calm way, steering your mind away from the grip of emotions or meaningless distractions, toward a more composed, purposeful state of mind.

The Heart is your true inner eye; it is what enables you to scan your mind for what is going on, and to move your mind to a state of peace and calm, once you teach it how. With a strong Heart, you become both more sympathetic to yourself, forgiving yourself for your errors, and you are also more self aware, able to access your strengths more easily.

We can, and will, still become unsettled when unpleasant or emotionally challenging things happen.

By taking time out to develop our attentiveness, we train the Heart in its role as an inner eye, to observe what is going on in our minds, settling and reassuring the upset mind, and allowing the wisdom and higher truths of life, shown to us by our own awareness, and the instructions from Allah, to guide us.

Being attentive gives us the ability choose what to be **aware** of. When things are overwhelming, an attentive mind says 'Hold on. Let's take a moment, take a breath, and give ourselves some time'.

This time turns out to be crucial in letting us deal with the emotion head on, as in Chapter 7, or in directing the information to our Intellect so we can question it a bit more, calmly, looking for evidence and facts to back it up. If we step back from an emotion, give it time to settle, then look at it more calmly, then we can get a better handle on it and create a better solution or a better course of action if we need to.

Observing our own mind, then, gives us the chance to **intervene**. Intervention is when we insert wisdom into our actions and reactions. It is what makes us more composed, it gives us a sense of perspective, reducing those mountains down back into molehills. It redirects us to our purposes and duties both materially and spiritually, as defined by the Intellect and Heart.

<u>Paying attention to your mind using the Heart</u>

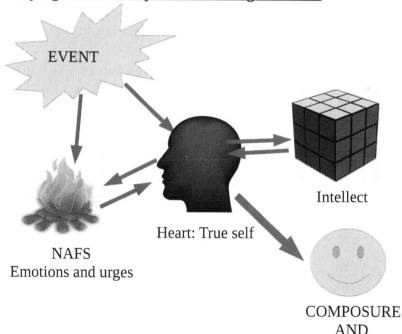

EVENT

Intellect

Heart: True self

NAFS
Emotions and urges

COMPOSURE
AND
WISE ACTION

We all know about wisdom, but we struggle to keep it foremost in our minds, to act on it when we really need to, before our impulses and poor judgments have taken hold. Wisdom and composure are the result of combining and choosing from of all aspects of our thinking: the task is to interrupt the Nafs before it hijacks our actions.

How to practice being attentive to the present moment

a) Remind ourselves of our purpose every day.

Every morning, try this:
- Revise your list of Rules of Conduct. Reflect on how you will show these values today.
- Write down a list of things you plan to get done today. Include at least one thing that you have been putting off.
- Write down three things that you are thankful for.
- Attend to your salah with a sense of gratitude and optimism that Allah has seen you and will help you along.

Every evening do this:
- Score off the list of things you got done. Thank Allah for the ability you showed today.
- Write a few lines about how your day went, reflecting on any emotionally noteworthy things: what do you learn about yourself, looking back?
- Jot down a few hopes and plans for the next few days.
- Reflect in your salah about how Allah helped you get your to-do list done, and asking for help in moving ahead.

b) Practice deep mindful reflection, or *Muraqabah: hearing Allah in the rhythm of your heart.*

Here is a ten-minute introduction to Muraqabah:

- Choose a quiet place to sit, away from distractions.
- Sit on the floor or on a chair, whatever is comfortable, with your back straight.
- Stare ahead on a fixed point in the middle distance, looking slightly beyond it, or close your eyes.
- Take slow, deep breaths in and out. Use your full chest. Concentrate on your breathing. Focus purely on this, as much as you can. Take time to enjoy getting it right.
- Repeat the process for a total of ten full breath cycles.
- Continue to breathe, then imagine the word 'Allah' slowly sounding at the pace of your heart beating. It might help if you want to say it out loud, softly, just under your breath.
- You might feel intrusion from distractions. This is OK. Simply invite your attention back to your breathing, and your inner rhythmic voice of *Allah.. Allah..Allah.*
- The Nafs will become quieter and more still, the more you do this.
- Let your mind wander if it wants to, but whatever you are feeling, whatever you are thinking, do not question its content: You are thankful to Allah for the opportunity to experience your mind and body in this way.
- You can end the process at any time; just count down from 10 breaths to zero.

Controlling your breathing and saying Allah with every heartbeat is like writing the words deeply in your Heart.

Deeply pious Muslims practice Muraqabah to the extent where remembrance of Allah is present in every single heartbeat, every single breath.

The Arabic word for deep, meditative reflection is called Muraqabah. In modern terms, the term is called 'Mindfulness', but the process has always been a very central practice of deeply pious Muslims who go on a journey to calm their Nafs and gain a sense of serene awareness over their mind and body. In ancient Arabic, the word murāqabah referred to one who would watch the night sky. It means 'observation'. Ancient Arabians would scan the sky in hopes to see the first signs of early stars to begin their journey.

Deep reflection can be a profoundly helpful process. It strengthens the Heart and helps a person become very closely connected to their purpose, their humanity, and they gain a great perspective of calmly understanding what is truly important.

There is nothing that is permanent in life; Allah has given us but the blink of an eye to exist. The best and the worst of people will all eventually pass into their grave; the most pressing problems of today will seem immaterial and forgotten, looking back. If we we had true insight, we would surely be far more attentive to our loved ones, less concerned with jobs, appearances and material distractions, and more focussed on finding solutions rather than dwelling on problems. Imagine being able to be in this state of mind more frequently: it would surely make us very wise, positive, and grounded. The benefits to the mind are enormous. Imagine being able to greet any event in life with the perspective of someone looking at life in completeness, with the consolation and company of Allah right by our side. Surely this is a very enlightened state of being.

Deep reflection is difficult to master, and is not a must. It is, however, a very helpful process when you accompany it with your efforts to achieve anything great in life, be it a material ambition, a wish to repair or improve a relationship with someone, or your wish to improve your understanding and insight of Deen on a more spiritual level. Those who do it more frequently find themselves more generous, more easy to be with, and more wise to the ways of the world, neither partaking of its temptations too much nor ignoring or rejecting it. The result is someone who is pleasant, grounded and positive to be around.

REFLECTIONS

When you control your pace of breathing,
Nobody can steal the pace of your life.

Take your time. At Allah's pace,
Even mountains are as temporary as clouds.

Don't paint the world with your interpretation:
Try to see it for what it is.

If you hear yourself with attention,
The noise eventually becomes exhausted.

SILENT and LISTEN are spelled with the same letters.

Anyone can count the seeds in an apple.
Those close to Allah see the apples within the seed.

Be still. Allah understands your prayers
Even when you don't have words to say them.

You might see Allah's work every day,
but only if you are attentive will you recognise it.

When you are thankful to Allah,
You are returning to Allah the flowers
He gave you at birth.

Chapter 11: Personality

Personality is a word to describe how you are individual as a person, in the way you think, feel and behave. You will remember from the tables in Chapter 3 and 4, that your Heart, Intellect and Nafs have a number of different qualities and functions, and people have different strengths in each.

Simply put, your personality is which of these elements has the strongest influence on your behaviour. In other words, your basic personality, and for that matter anyone else's basic personality, is made up of which of these qualities are most often on display.

Here's a simple way to work out someone's basic personality.
1. How strong is the Heart? (Beliefs, Deen, conduct)
2. What is the dominant emotional makeup? (Nafs)
3. How much is their Intellect in evidence?(Roles and abilities).

The Personality in the Heart

This comes first and foremost because the a person with strong Heart has dominion over Intellect and Nafs. How much is this person aware of what is going on around them, and calm in a storm? How effective are they at achieving their purposes and roles in life? How much do they show good conduct regardless of stress? How much do they understand and practise Deen?

A strong Heart leads to a principled personality, not worried about whether others notice: the only judges are your conscience and Allah.

Next, we look at our Intellect and Nafs. To do this, think about how you are, and now tick which ones of these qualities are uppermost in your nature. Tick three on each side. Six in total.

Emotional- Nafs	Tick	Intellectual	Tick
Safety		Logic and reason win above emotions	
Status and respect		Needing to know facts and figures	
Having nice things		Doing what's morally right regardless	
Bonding and loyalty		Being fair even if it means you lose out	
Easily ruffled		Preferring to do things the same way every time	
Sensitive ego		Planning things carefully before doing them	
Being competitive and victorious is crucial		Missing the point of things that other people get easily	
Able to sense danger very well; not readily trusting		Tends to give trust without judging the person first	
Worried about reputation		Unaware when they are being boring or argumentative	
Can't resist small temptations			
Focussed on fathering or mothering role			

Done it? Now you have a few of your most important personality forces. You can do this for yourself, or someone you know fairly well.

When you know these things, you can more easily understand how to get along with a person. Bear this in mind:
1. If their Heart is dominant, then they will be easier to get along with and a force for good.
2. Everyone has an active Nafs. Knowing what style of Nafs they have will give you a clue as to what you can do to please them. For example, if they are very focussed on material possessions, you can win favour by giving them a carefully thought gift which is to their taste. If they are more interested in status and respect, you can take care to show that you respect their position.

It is true to say that most people's basic personality is formed from these things, in order from the lowest to the most important:

- **a) Temperament:** their natural tendencies, observable even when they were infants: calm, nervous, secure, etc. Their Nafs has a particular affinity for certain traits.

- **b) Upbringing:** the first 8 years or so are formative in a fairly permanent way on how the person will be later in life

- **c) Significant events:** traumas in particular, can bring about dramatic change. Traumas have an effect of unleashing parts of the Nafs. Some people who have gone through trauma are unchanged, but some are more frightened, emotionally unstable and angry, while others seem to be more detached and focussed, perhaps even more productive, as a result of trauma. Think how it has affected you.

- **d) Intellect:** which of their particular intelligences is prominent, and whether they have developed and capitalised on their particular Intellect, giving themselves value and skill.

- **e) Self awareness:** If a person develops their Heart, becoming more aware and nurturing of their purpose, their conduct and their faith, this can transform their personality for the better at any stage in their life.

Personality is not permanent, nor is it consistent. We have a degree of insight into how we are, but this changes over time, and our perception of ourselves can even be different depending on where and when we are asked about it. Learning about our own personality is something that again takes effort and reflection over time. We gain a lot from this process, but we gain just as much from learning about other people around us. One of the most important purposes we have is to be of service and benefit to the people who matter to us; by understanding their personality more, we can fulfil our role towards them more effectively and peacefully.

REFLECTIONS

Aim to be the best version of yourself.
It's better than trying to be a poor imitation of others.

Work with what you are. If Allah had wanted you
otherwise, He would have created you as someone
else.

The only time you are permitted
to look down on someone,
Is when you are helping them up.

Growing to be what you are also includes mourning
For the things you cannot be.

Resolve to find and refine your identity;
The quest itself will strengthen you.

We are all born as originals,
And yet we try to become copies.

Allah won't ask why you weren't a saint.
He will ask why you weren't yourself.

Trim yourself once, to fit someone you truly value;
Make sure there is plenty of you left over though.

You are a grain of sand.
You need others around if you want to make a beach.

INSTANT INSIGHTS

Chapter 12: Relationships- Inner Circle

Two types of relationship with our inner circle can be defined:

a) Your family and close friends
b) Your partner

Your Family

Your family (and sometimes, your closest friends) are your **tribe**, as far as your Nafs is concerned, and Allah has given us instincts of loyalty to tribe and family which are binding upon us in terms of our conduct and security. Alhamdulillah, this is a great positive quality of the Nafs. Human beings are social, and bonded, and those who are bonded as a tribe have the asset of loyalty, which makes them guard, forgive, and provide for people within their close circle.

We must take heed and obey our parents; they are senior to us, and they are therefore accorded loyalty and respect. When we are young they have full authority over us, and as we get older, we might converse, persuade and negotiate with them more, but the respect must remain prime. It is far better to err towards obedience to our parents because their own Nafs will be inclined to see us as lower and subservient to them, and their bond to us always requires us to acknowledge this to some extent. As we get older, this drive diminishes, and we might even find ourselves guiding our parents. Regardless of this, we must retain and emphasise a sense of respect for parents' views.

Even if we deeply disagree, or if they do something morally unacceptable, we must fulfil our duty to be at least civil and available to them, while humbly stating our case with honesty: loyalty is maintained by communication and respect, even when disagreement exists. Allah tells us so, and there is much good in this.

We have **role** with our family and close friends which is influenced both by Nafs and Heart; we can be defender, protector, nurturer, provider, guardian, ally and servant. We must listen to ourselves and be glad to follow these positive instincts if and when they are useful to these important people. It gives us value and strength to do so. The Intellect, as ever, is important as problem solver, planner, and executor of duties.

Arguments in the family

We must also be mindful of the Nafs when it comes to close connections; it can indeed become out of control. Jealousies may fester, there will be rivalries for authorities and power between siblings, or people become resentful of wealth or assets that others in the family have. Arguments can and will break out.

Where this happens in family, we must not react to emotion with emotion. It is always better to remain calm, walk away and give yourself time for your Intellect and Heart to show up. Once they do, you can consider things using your ability to think logically and step by step using your Intellect, and use your Heart to think about what greater wisdom and consolation there is to be had.

Remember also the role of humour: the fascinating thing about humour is that it allows us to acknowledge a truth by making light of how we are all prone to errors.

Finding a good resolution can be achieved if we communicate with family with three things in mind: **right time, right place, and right person.** The solution to a dispute is unlikely to be reached when emotions are already high; we must consider carefully when, where, and with whom we should discuss the issues at hand.

Because family will always be with us, we have a duty of honesty to them which is higher than normal: if they err, we must find the right time, right place, and right person to talk to, frankly and honestly. We must hope that they will do the same.

We must be open to others in our circle being very frank with us when we fall short, allowing them licence to speak to us frankly when they appear calm and intent on helping us to correct our behaviour.

Your partner
In deciding how we pair up with our life partner, we nowadays have a lot more freedom than in the past. Indeed, Islam has always taught us to give both men and women the choice as to who they decided partner with, and also gives them the forum to do so: we have ways in which we can get to know our potential partners in a decent and dignified way.

164

Partnering with a spouse can be described in three phases:
* Romantic attraction
* Companionship
* Commitment

It does not matter which order these things happen in. Westernised cultures place a value on the romantic attraction first, followed by companionship and then commitment, but in most non-Western cultures, the order is completely reversed: a bride and groom are first married, then they become companions though being with each other, then finally they experience blossomings of romantic love.

The best compromise might be, in fact, to try companionship first. Companionship, duly observed in a halal way, allows a man and woman to look into each others' character with a degree of safety, respect and cordiality. However, as long as the method of pairing is halal, and there participants are willing, Allah does not demand us to follow any specific order.

Deciding suitability: What are you incompatible with?

To find out about who we are compatible with, it is a good idea to turn the idea of compatibility upside down: to look at who we would **not** be compatible with. For this, we look at the Nafs or emotional domain most closely. If someone else's particular emotions and desires are particularly irksome or troubling for you, it can be very difficult for your own Nafs to feel bonded to them.

If you were to think about the potential partner, and list the 3 elements of their Nafs that are most important, then it would be best if you were able to tolerate all three without any sense of discomfort. You might even have the same traits. However, if even one of those three things is unacceptably irritating or troubling to you, then you are going to find it tricky to get along with them. This is because the Nafs is a tough and stubborn element of us that we have to accept: we each have a Nafs is within our own nature, which we try to control and adapt to, but which cannot be changed readily. The basic emotional outlook is difficult to change: we are who we are.

And this is the key: when you are with a loved one, you will need every day to walk a line which both acknowledges their Nafs, and appeases it, in order to keep it calm and happy. To do so, by reciprocation, calms and settles your own Nafs.

Putting their needs ahead of yours.

Success in a relationship is also about **how much two people can put the other person's needs ahead of their own,** forming a roughly equal picture of give and take. This takes effort; it takes energy, but if you can do it without getting exhausted, and that you find you are at peace from having been of service to them, then your Nafs is in line with theirs. Inshallah, if they have the same approach to you, accepting your emotional foibles and catering to them without making you feel awkward or demanding, then you have found a good partner.

166

In a thriving partnership, each partner wakes every day with a question: **what can I do today to make my partner happy?** This surely require us to understand each other's emotions and desires, and cater to them with happy effort, thereby helping them to settle their own Nafs as much as they settle ours.

In effect we can probably get along with 3 in every 4 people we meet, finding something in common, to like and value, in most people. If we all matched in terms of our Nafs, then there would be no particular reason to be loyal to the people we were close to. In essence, we develop loyalty, bonding, and element of *irrational closeness: LOVE*, for those whose faults or quirks we can tolerate, or that we have in common. If the other person has visible and present tendencies of the Nafs that annoy or confuse us, then these will only become more troubling over time, no matter how much we get along in other ways.

Attending to each others' emotions

Keeping a relationship going requires active effort and habits that are developed specifically to signify that you treasure that person over and above their basic role.

Try to understand which parts of their Nafs are most obvious. Then, think of ways that acknowledge and appease those parts in a measured way. The Nafs responds to recognition, remember.

For example, if your wife has a strong maternal drive, giving up her other interests to focus on the children, then think of ways to remind her of how she truly shines in that role with the children; regular flowers and thanks are rarely underappreciated. But also remind her that you can help with the children so that she can return to some of the other things she liked doing, otherwise her mothering Nafs would dominate her so much that she becomes utterly dispirited and exhausted. Whatever the part of the Nafs is on show, it needs validation: a person with loyalty needs to be reminded and thanked for it; a person with insecurity about their status needs reassurance that they are respected.

The Intellect in your partner helps them to form their own individual roles and goals: it should be your goal to encourage this to shine, because it helps your partner to feel fulfilled and masterful. Using your Intellect, and relying on your Heart, will help you both to move forward, dividing up duties and moving together towards living more from faith and good conduct as you both grow. Even for those of strong Heart, the Nafs is ever present, and if they are our partner, then we must cater to it.

The role of the Heart

Just as much as we can measure our own and others' personalities by the strength of their Heart, so it is that we must look to the Heart in our partner too. Allah tells us to look closely into someone's character-: their Heart, or True self, when choosing a partner. There is excellent reasoning for this. A person's true, developed character can be seen in how much they are able to carry out their roles and responsibilities with purpose and wisdom. The strong Heart demonstrates good rules of conduct especially when facing stressful, new, or emotionally provocative territory. It is wise, therefore, to consider how someone copes with difficulty: if they remain loyal to their loved ones and show reluctance to be destructive or impulsive, then this is indeed a very admirable individual.

These elements are what signify a person who is truly on a fast track of success. It is important to note that you should try to match with someone as to where they are in matters of faith, and to be sure that they, like you, are on the journey of improving the True Self in all of its functions as time goes on.

Looks, power, and money

Romantic attraction is a confusing feeling, because it is a part of the Nafs. It is difficult, especially for younger people, to distinguish temporary attraction from a truer sense of worth. The Nafs has a way of instant affinity with some things such as appearance, power and wealth. These may have their uses, but you should think for yourself as to what these things really mean. They have little relevance to Heart, and in fact, they are a burden and responsibility to carry that many do not succeed with.

Having attractive appearance, or wealth and power, is a difficult thing to manage. If you have these apparent gifts, people will be more easily attracted to you, and more likely to do your bidding, but they are driven by their Nafs. As a result they are also less consistent, and possibly less trustworthy, being interested in these assets rather than in your Heart.

Being blessed with these things is therefore as much of a test as any other, and it will indeed be harder for you to be patient and to develop your character if you are constantly eased or distracted by the short-cuts afforded you by such superficial qualities as money or good looks.

The reality is that Heart: your true nature and strength, is something that is entirely up to you to nurture and develop. This is why it is better to look at a person's morality, actions, and faith, as a better sign of their quality than the rather spurious and transient gifts like looks and money. We are gravely cautioned against excess wealth by Allah, because it breeds corruption and impatience, and seduces us into seeking all our fulfilment from material comforts. Looks and wealth are, in reality, very random things, that are mere incidents of circumstance; each can arrive, and be taken away, instantly.

REFLECTIONS

Be grateful for the loved ones who depend on you.
Serving them gives you a hold on the meaning of life.

Listen to the victories and losses of your loved ones.
Sharing joy doubles it, while sharing sorrow halves it.

Assumptions and expectations are like termites
Feeding on the beams of your relationships.

In families, one of the magic words is 'please'.
The other one is 'sorry'.

The greatest gift at a family gathering is the family,
And the gathering.

A marriage consists of two spouses, two slaves, and
Two rulers, making a total of two.

Being alone can be too cold. Unrequited love, too hot.
Marriage is at body temperature.

Don't smother your spouse.
No plant can grow well hidden in your shade.

A happy marriage is a long conversation
Where both know what not to say.

INSTANT INSIGHTS

Chapter 13. Relationships- Outer Circle

In connecting with other people, we use our Intellect to:
- understand other people before seeking to be understood ourselves.
- allow others to express themselves without investing in their emotional life.
- stay close to the truths, facts and the logic in our dealing with others
- look for solutions in life rather than dwell on problems and negatives.

The Hadith- words of the Prophet- tell us that a person is known by the friends that they have. Select your friends carefully, and choose people other than those who have a negative impact on you.

The Hadith also remind us that we should be limited in the amount that we disclose to friends: to trust friends in moderation. Friends might take us for granted, or if our friendship with them breaks, then they might be tempted to talk badly of us if we have entrusted them with things that might be damaging to us were they revealed to others.

You might feel that this is a strangely cautionary place from which to talk about friendship. This book is not so much about the ideal world as it is about the real world. A person with strong Heart will understand that we need friends; they are an important part of lives, a great asset, and a great source of support.

However, we also need to know that friendship is a relationship, which is transmitted along three lines as always: Nafs, Intellect, and Heart. Out of these,

- be careful of the Nafs- both yours and theirs
- try to use the Intellect in your dealings with them
- and seek the Heart to find the finest of them

The Nafs in its extreme would have us associate with people who are there for good times alone, being as it is driven by the quest for pleasure. Quick thrills and temptations are not a way to base a true friendship on; true friends emerge when they are happy to be bored alongside us, and present when we are having a difficult time. If a friend is a gambler, an addict, or someone who routinely talks ill of others, or lives in a way that is fundamentally unhappy with themselves and the people around them, we should know to keep our distance.

In our social groupings, we must recognise the capacity of the Intellect and Heart. They invite us to

- enjoy doing things together by mutual cooperation
- deal with different opinions by listening and compromising
- show respect and compassion in a friendly way
- seek to be likeable, but not worry whether we are liked.
- see others as responsible for their happiness and their duties
- choose others based on their qualities rather than their appearance or their power.

If a person is being very friendly towards you, this is not enough reason to become their friend. Think about it: would you be super-friendly to a stranger without reason? Those people who make you feel as if you are the only one who is important to them, and reveal secrets to you too early on, are better off kept at arm's length.

Friends bond with each other when we are children, often through nothing more than we spend time with them in the same place. As we grow, some of those friendships will last the test of time and separation, and are often the strongest: the bond of childhood friendship is made when the Nafs and Intellect are yet innocent, at play. If your Heart develops alongside a friend's, then that friend will be among the strongest of all.

Circles of closeness

Closest: spouse and family

Good friends

Familiar acquaintances

Strangers

13. RELATIONSHIPS- OUTER CIRCLE
Good friends

The closest friends usually only number one or two. It is most important that those friends are good of Heart: they are in touch with their true selves, and live life with good purpose, are good in their knowledge and practice of faith, and conduct themselves in a way that would make us proud of being their friend. In essence, we must try to choose friends who are positive company for us, who put us foremost in their thoughts, and who do things that we would be proud of because they are our friends.

By return, we must invest in them too, making sure that we are there for them, showing them that we are thinking of them, and doing things that would make them proud of us. This takes a lot of effort, which is why we do not have so many of these friends. If we are fortunate and wise, those friends would also have similarity in their outlook on life, perhaps with similar instincts and tendencies: they instinctively understand us and we them.

Familiar friendly acquaintances

The second circle is that group whom we know to be good people, but we are not close to them in terms of sharing secrets; we might have friendly social exchanges with them, and be involved at some group level, and we might rely on them in some social exchanges such as business leads, or help with school. They are our friendly circle of our outer social sphere, and work-related people.

We keep them at arm's length: this is perfectly good and proper, and ensures that we build trust and rapport with them in a steady way, over time, before we entrust them with too much. Even then we must always observe and learn about them, checking the way they conduct themselves, how honest and dependable and good natured they are, before deciding consciously whether we want a closer friendship. This is a wisdom of reality.

At work, we rely on Intellect to form the plans and actions that move an organisation or business forward. This is the extent of where we should go. It is good and proper for us to work together with other people for a worldly cause, business or profession. It is not wise, though, for us to take too much by way of emotional support, or offer it either, to the world of work. Unfortunately, those of us who do this will find that what you give will not be returned, leading us to become disillusioned or exhausted.

Strangers

The further out the circle, the more cautious we ought to be. We must remain friendly and open, but be vigilant especially to the intentions of people who would be too keen to befriend us, perhaps telling us too much about themselves, or being too complimentary towards us.

If we see that an acquaintance is unable to restrain their own inner Nafs, disclosing too much about themselves, or being too familiar, then we should indeed be extra careful around them.

You are not responsible for the happiness, actions, and attitudes of friendly acquaintances, strangers and others outside your close circle. You must demonstrate good character but exercise your generosity with care and caution. You are only responsible for your own words and behaviour, and your own health and wellbeing. You are partly responsible for the happiness of your loved ones and your partner because you have formed an investment in their full existence, including their emotional needs: the contract with them is much closer, and with good reason. They will be with you and there for you much more than any workplace or acquaintance will.

The role of jobs, work and career

No matter how important work is, it should rarely if ever be more important than family. We must commit time to work and earning, but be mindful about balancing it with genuine attention to how well we are doing in the other equally important jobs we have for life: as fathers, mothers, sons, daughters and siblings.

There are many books and guides on how to be more productive, how to win friends and influence people, how to make more money, and what have you. As Muslims, we are better off knowing that none of this should be taken to be too central in our lives.

Sure, it is worthy to be productive, because it is important to know that we have something that we can contribute with, that we are skilled for, and that we can get paid for.

It is halal and proper to participate in commerce. However, we do not subscribe to the more fervent pressures of endless commerce, with its obsessions with ownership, wealth and growth. We must strive for *enough*, and be deeply sceptical of having *too much*. If we do have too much, we must hasten to give it away in a way that is wise and productive for its recipients.

For workaholic men in particular, they erroneously tell themselves that they are working to earn money because their Nafs' urge to provide security and safety has overtaken their better judgment: in reality, no matter what you think, your family requires more of your finest attention than your work.

It is a shame that so many people frame their best behaviour and thoughtfulness for times when they are at work, assuming that family will just understand and grow without their attention. They are either groggy and irritable in the morning, or exhausted and irritable at night, unable to give of their best to their loved ones. This is hazardous. Keep in mind your higher purposes, and your obligations and roles, as defined by your Deen and kept in your Heart. Work must be balanced out by home life, and in particular, your mental capacities and character must be at their best when you are with your family, even more so than at work. Your family needs you more than your work does. Allah tells us so.

Your wife should not be a widow to your work, your sports or your hobbies. Time spent teaching and playing with your children should never be an afterthought after your demanding work schedule or socialising with the boss. Your work will rarely if ever treat you with the loyalty of true family, despite whatever promises, mottos and working culture are present.

The Nafs does indeed have a use at work, particularly when dealing with large numbers of people, or when facing strangers. The Nafs gives you a sense of caution and alertness to non-verbal cues: the 'sixth sense' of judging what the emotional atmosphere is like. This is part of what is known as 'emotional intelligence'.

Emotional intelligence is the ability to tune into how people are feeling and to use this to navigate your way through work without upsetting people, by winning their favour. This means do use your Nafs to sense the emotional environment, to judge when and whom to speak to, to react deftly to colleagues or customers' needs. This makes you far more successful than those who simply rely on technical ability. This should get better the more you practice reflection and self awareness, providing you also reflect on such experiences in your own time.

Accomplishing crazy feats at work only means that
Your boss adds them to your regular duties.

The closest friends are those who ask how you are
And then listen for an honest answer.

If people seem suspicious,
It's usually because you are right.

Trust only actions.
Life happens in movement, not words.

Be trustworthy, and declare that you expect the same.

Unwise are those weigh the injuries they cause
On different scales than the ones they suffer.

Seek good character in yourself;
You will recognise it more easily in others.

If unemployment means time to plant your own
garden, you're doing something right.

People are never happy with their salary because
Once it goes up, they raise their own expenses.

If you feel inadequate without gold and silver,
You will still be inadequate when you are with them.

INSTANT INSIGHTS

Chapter 14: Confidence

Confidence is the thing that most people want to improve. Alhamdulillah, there are many ways to understand confidence, and master it.

Confidence is troublesome when people worry about **being good** at something. This causes a lot of anxiety.

Confidence comes from **doing your best**. It is not about being good as such.

If you think about this properly for a minute, you will see what is meant here. You can only control what you **do** in life. You cannot control the result: maybe it will turn out you are at your best, maybe it will turn out you are not. If you apply yourself and simply do your best, managing as best you can, then you will get the best possible result on the day.

Being good at something is a *result*- an *outcome*. Outcomes and results are not predictable. Every outcome is different, every time. No wonder people get anxious about it: results are not within our control.

Doing your best is different: it is about simply applying yourself as best you can. This is within your control. Whatever limitations you have on the day, whatever the circumstances are that are for or against you, whatever the weather, you can do your best on the day, every day. Whether you are good at the task is really up to Allah. Confidence comes from understanding this.

It is also wrong to think that having anxiety means a lack of confidence. This is also wrong. It is perfectly okay to feel fear and trepidation about doing something. A small amount of anxiety from the Nafs, warning us to stay alert, is useful in a measured amount, because the body's senses quicken and we become more focussed. Confidence lies in using that force to perform better; without any anxiety at all we would not be focussed on the task at hand.

In situations when we are overwhelmed by fear, it is better to take a step back and calm our Nafs. We can only ever put our effort into something: the results of our efforts are up to Allah.

Alhamdulillah, Allah has designed us to be as we are: given to temptations, self doubt, and imperfection. This is part of our journey on Earth. We need to begin to believe that we can only give our best effort, as broken and inadequate as it might be, regardless of what our doubts or preconceptions are.
It is only through this that we can then become more confident, because we are being optimistic and realistic, and living in the present moment. *Results* are only really in the future, or the past. *Efforts* are in the present.

The Nafs has a strong impact on our confidence. Commonly, the Nafs gives us a variable signal: sometimes we can feel motivated and brave, other times we can feel crippled by anxiety.

Most often when it comes to doing something difficult, the Nafs gets anxious. It is worried about what others will think if we fail, and therefore stops us from trying to be adventurous and positive. It also believes that failing at something will make us failures as people- the error of 'all or nothing' thinking.

Sometimes, the Nafs gets over-exuberant. It is so anxious to show off to others that it tempts us to take risks doing things we are unable to do. It is so anxious to prove its worth that it believes that our self-worth lies in succeeding at one thing alone. Both of these are also misleading and troublesome.

If we rely on the Nafs, then we become unduly confident or under-confident.

The rope bridge

Supposing you were in front of a rope bridge.

The bridge is long, and at a great height. You have been told that it is absolutely safe to cross, as long as you just keep hold of the ropes and tread on the wooden boards.

186

You have also been given a safety harness which attaches your body very securely: if you lose your grip, or fall, the safety harness will prevent you from falling. No harm will come to you, and people will immediately come to your aid quickly. You are the first in line to go across; others are behind you, waiting to do the same task right after you. Everyone is nervous; some are excitable.

Many of us would feel fear and anxiety at this prospect, despite the reassurances. Why should this be so? The Nafs has a lot to do with the answer. There are a couple of reasons:

1. *Negative salience.*

The Nafs has a self-preservation instinct, which tends to look at things in terms of what could go wrong, rather than what could go right. Because the Nafs is as strong and as quick as it is, we jump to the conclusion that we are not going to succeed. The Nafs would have us imagining that we are going to fall; visions of being hurt and worse come flooding in.

2. *Group effects.*

a) *Emotions are contagious:* The Nafs is very much driven to feel the way the rest of the group are feeling. Confidence is contagious, and so is a lack of confidence. When we are around others who feel a certain way about something, we are naturally inclined to feel the same way, without examining the evidence for the feeling.

b) *Groups exaggerate attitudes.*

We become even more put off something if others are put off. When we are with others, the attitude we have to a task is amplified many times, to agree with what the group thinks. If someone influential in the group decides that something is risky, then others follow that cue: the feeling becomes intensified much more than if just one person was thinking the matter through on their own. If everyone is massively afraid of the task, then even those who were initially unafraid begin to feel afraid, and this then transmits back to others, making the attitude even stronger. Incidentally, the same thing applies to when the group feel confident about something: people can become foolhardy and dive into dangerous waters because others are doing so. The point is that neither of these is accurate or based on actual evidence. It is all just impressions and feelings- the domain of the Nafs.

3. *All-or-nothing thinking.*

We have this idea of crossing the bridge in a single manoeuvre. We imagine the whole event being succeeded or failed in one step. This is, of course, wrong.

Our emotions inhibit our Intellect to actually see the task for what it is: a series of very small steps.

To tackle the problem, we would have to consider

- A. Dealing with anxious nerves directly
- B. Calling on the Intellect to help us through the task logically
- C. Listening to the wisdoms and truths in the Heart.

Calming yourself quickly and directly

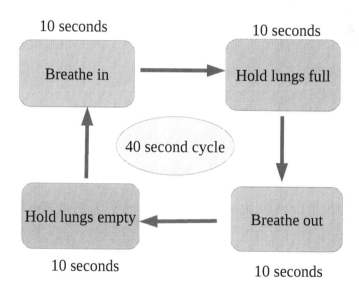

Focus only on your breathing.
Every step should take 10 seconds:
a) breathing in, b) holding the lungs full, c) breathing out,
d) holding the lungs empty. This is a 40 second cycle.

If you can't manage ten seconds, try shorter times. This process reduces the amount of excess oxygen in your body, and also stimulates the key nerves that control your breathing and heart rate to slow down. Go round the cycle as many times as you need to: the more you practice it, the better you will get at reducing your emotional overload. This in turn also improves the blood circulation to your frontal lobes: where your logical thinking (Intellect) resides.

Using the Intellect to become more confident

1. *Examine the evidence.* There is no possibility of getting hurt, because there is reassurance from the safety harness and we also learn that nobody has ever gotten hurt crossing the bridge.

2. *Breaking the task down, and planning how to do it.* The Intellect is happiest when it is asked to break things down into manageable steps. It enjoys sequences and procedures, each of which is successful on its own. Sequences and procedures add up to become the whole effort. The bridge can only be crossed one little step at a time.

Somehow, this isn't enough for many people. They are still irrationally and inescapably afraid of stepping out into that scary space. It seems as if the Nafs is still dominating their feelings. They imagine being the first person to fall off the bridge in its history, as unlikely as that seems! So, this is where the Heart, with its wisdom and higher guidance, can help us.

Confidence from the Heart
Wisdoms of Deen

Alhamdulillah. What can we really do to prevent our destiny? Nothing. We just do the best we can in life to aim for our goals; our destiny is outside our control.

Allah says we are not to be concerned with the results of our efforts: that is up to Him. We are only in control of the efforts we put in. Every single thing we do is acknowledged and monitored by Allah. If by some bizarre accident we are the first to ever fall off that bridge why fear such an unlikely thing? It would be the same to walk around fearing that we are about to be struck by lightning, or a stray meteor. Allah encourages us to accept our lives, being as cautious as we reasonably can, taking care not to hide from the world.

Truths of life
The useful Truth in this case is that *the present moment is the only one we can control.* If we want a good future in 5 seconds' time, or in 5 days' time, this can only happen if we take care of this moment right now. So when we are crossing the bridge, we pay close attention just to the very thing we are doing at that moment: getting that next step right, steadying our hands on the rope, and then moving forward step by step.

Rules of Conduct
We have decided as a way of life, to be hopeful, and cheerful.

The more we remember our Rules of Conduct every day, and put them into use every day, the more they become a part of our character, and the more we will succeed. It is a fact that people who approach things more positively will do them better. This positivity is best if it is something that comes from deep within-something that they keep sacred, that they have nurtured and reminded themselves about. Allah enjoys your positivity.

Confidence and courage

Sometimes in life, we face such enormous tasks that our anxieties are way too high. The situation might be urgent; we cannot take time out because life and death is at stake. We can still be confident. Here's how:

a) Confidence comes from simply doing our best. Even if the odds are against us, we can be confident in setting out to live within our limitations, accept them, and do our best anyway. The effort is ours, the results are up to Allah.

b) Anxiety is not to be confused for a lack of courage. It is a myth to think that courageous people lack fear. People who lack fear in the face of adversity are are foolhardy. True courage comes from feeling fear, and taking action anyway.

Confidence and competence

The rope bridge is a good symbol of many of the things we set out to do in life.

If you were a professional climber, the rope bridge would seem simple enough- no problem whatsoever. In life, if we are going to become very good at something, we must practise, and expect to learn slowly, incrementally, making mistakes along the way as we all do. Only then do we become masterful at anything. Our job is to turn up at life: to decide what we want to do, and then apply ourselves as best we can, using our Intellect to plan and practise, and our Heart as the source of wisdom and purpose.

The professional climber's problem

Consider this: a professional mountain climber is at the bridge, and is terrified of crossing. He is physically completely fit, yet he is still afraid. Why might this be?

When we have practised at something, our confidence is more likely to be accurate and justified. There are times when this is not the case though. Whilst it is true that becoming more competent at something makes us more confident, other factors also come into play. Recent experiences, or knowledge of our limitations and specialism, may still limit our confidence.

a) *Recent experiences.* He might have recently had an accident, falling off a side of a mountain. Technically he can do the task, but his Nafs is irrationally preoccupied with his accident.

b) *Having very specific skills.* He might be a professional mountain climber, and happily climb any mountain, but he may not know anything about rope bridges. He therefore has no memory or conception of whether he will succeed in the crossing, and is therefore as scared as anyone else. Ability and expertise in one area of life does not automatically mean ability in another.

Many mountain climbers are in fact scared of heights: they climb mountains because of the pleasure they get from conquering this fear: an adrenaline high that comes from having studied the art of climbing carefully and applied it to their effort. They can climb the mountain, as anyone ever does, one footstep and one hand grip at a time. They have never crossed a rope bridge: it might seem similar, but not similar enough for them to feel able to cross.

<u>Confidence and self awareness</u>

Feeling confident about something, or not, is a misleading thing. Emotions and impressions are merely estimations of a situation, and they are frequently wrong. The Nafs is a blunt instrument: it may trick us into extremes: feeling very over-confident, or lacking confidence altogether. Neither of these is really helpful in the long term. Many people are not confident at doing something, yet turn out to be very good at it. Others may believe they will be very good at something, and turn out to be terrible at it.

It is far better to approach tasks trying our best, rather than expecting ourselves to succeed or fail. Allah has asked us to stray towards the positive side a little bit: to have hope, and to be cheerful and thankful for the opportunity to do something. The effort is up to us; the result is not.

194

We take responsibility for our actions, and deal with the consequences as they come. **Neither success nor failure are to be celebrated or mourned too much: neither is our master.**

Of course, it is useful to try to educate and tame our Nafs, understanding our emotions and finding ways to attend to them, and diffuse them, as we grow. It is important, then, to educate it: to allow it to express emotions, but to also diffuse unnecessary emotions by thinking things though, and reflecting on our experiences, talking to Allah about what we learn about ourselves and the world as we go along (chapter 9). This is the act of becoming self aware. The more we do this, the more we gain a sense of mastery over ourselves.

Emotions are not something to be excluded, locked away, and suppressed from our activities and endeavours. It is wiser to deal with them gently and intelligently.

For example, when we do succeed at something, we must make effort to celebrate it. Taking that first step onto the bridge is such an example of success: we must celebrate that: it calms the Nafs immensely. It settles the emotions, and reduces the impact of excessive anxiety. Every single change in life creates a small amount of anxiety: this is the state of our *insaaniyat*.

We must be sympathetic to this, and take time to celebrate every small success. We rarely stumble over mountains: we stumble over small rocks.

Acknowledging the success of others is also a great deed: the Nafs does seek validation and acknowledgement from others, and is settled when such acknowledgement is given.

When we are deciding on what to do with our lives, we must also consider how to use and deal with the Nafs: it is a powerful force for progress, or a great impediment to it, depending on how we deal with it. We will consider this in the next chapter: succeeding in your goals.

14. CONFIDENCE

REFLECTIONS

Let your confidence stem from your effort,
Rather than your expectation of success.

Confidence is expecting that you will make mistakes
As lessons in bettering yourself.

If you argue why you can't do something difficult,
You have decided the outcome without trying.

When your first venture fails you learn that the sky
doesn't fall down. At that point, you gain confidence.

Your appeal lies half in what you have,
And half in what other people think you have.

Your actual capabilities are always greater
Than your ability to exploit them.

You have your limitations, but if you listen
To others' criticisms, you will also have theirs.

One of Allah's mercies is when he gifts you
The power to get something you ask Him for.

You can harm others with your actions,
But you can harm yourself with your own thoughts.

INSTANT INSIGHTS

Chapter 15: Motivation

The role of motivation

People often describe a lack of motivation when they are trying to achieve something. Commitment is better than motivation: Commitment comes from a plan to do something regardless of how good or bad you feel about it on any given day. Commitment is followed up with humility and tiny steps: We all make the mistake of staring at the peak of the mountain, not at the few steps in front of us. Every single goal is just a series of tiny steps, one by one. Commitment sees us through to following these steps. Motivation is not effective in helping us to be consistent in the way commitment is.

People have plenty of motivation in the beginning, they seem to have run out half way through. They become bewildered and frustrated, somehow unable to continue towards their goal. Why should this be?

Motivation is a feeling, and as such, it is a temporary and often transient thing.

Motivation is a part of the Nafs: the motivation you feel when you really want to achieve something good, to score a goal in football, or to beat someone in an argument. These things are motive forces, which map onto some kind of drive to demonstrate success. The feeling is useful for a short period only, and then it is gone.

Occasional pep-talks can give your motivation refreshment, and so pep-talks are used by coaches in half-time talks with their teams, and by salespeople before they embark on a gruelling door-to-door selling effort.

But for all long-term goals, meaning anything that takes longer than a day to achieve, pure emotional motivation is unreliable, and inconsistent, and not of as much worth as we expect it to be. It is best to consider motivation as coming to us in a series of moments, where we can take time out to inspire ourselves with higher meaning or anticipation of reward, or comfort ourselves with greater wisdoms when we are feeling weary.

Commitment is more powerful than motivation

Commitment is superior to motivation, because commitment is a contract to undertake tasks toward your goal in a clear and unshakeable way, without being hampered by how you feel. Commitment comes from your Heart and your Intellect. The Heart defines your conduct and keeps your purpose and mission clear, calming and interrupting the Nafs when negative emotions are excessive. The Intellect defines your plan, and your day to day strategy to get to your goal.

Handling the Nafs is important. We must acknowledge the Nafs and accept our feelings, but also be sympathetic and give it rewards in terms of little victories: these are really satisfying for the Nafs. In other words, celebrate reaching small targets. Refresh your Nafs with exercise, play, and stretching.

Goals are achieved by breaking them down into a series of reachable targets. At each point, we must celebrate the achievement, calming the Nafs. We must also, at each point, reflect on how the target has advanced us forward, taking steps to adjust our course if we need to.

REFLECTIONS

INSTANT INSIGHTS

Motivation helps you take off.
Commitment gives you landing gear.

Turn up to your plans:
It is the only way you can do your ambition justice.

When you fail and the world doesn't end,
You realise that fear is merely a tool, not an obstacle.

If you have pride, let it be in the fact
That you are too proud to stop trying.

He conquers who simply endures.

Rain carves the rocks not by strength
But by insistence.

If you truly remember what you succeed in every day,
Then you will have little cause to stop going.

The postage stamp succeeds
Because it sticks with something all the way.

Commitment is the knot you tie in your rope
So that you can hang on if you slide to the end of it.

Allah gives you big dreams
Only because he wants you to grow into them.

INSTANT INSIGHTS

Chapter 16: Success

Alhamdulillah. Provided that you are in touch with your faith, positivity, and self awareness, Allah will surely help you to achieve success.

Success comes from having a sense of purpose, and from achieving goals that are directed to that purpose. Whether you know it or not, you have purposes and goals, and achieve them all the time. If you have a brother, your purpose is to be a good sibling to him. If you want to eat something, you go and eat it. If you want to go outside, you do so. We are far more successful than we like to think: we tend to take our small achievements for granted. And here is the good news:

All big achievements are the result of many small achievements towards a greater goal.

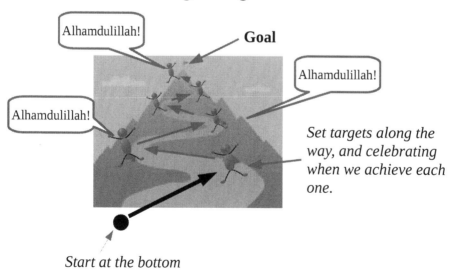

We have many purposes, related to our many roles.

Alhamdulillah, we have guidance from Allah on our purposes in this world: to be useful and good to ourselves and others, and to please Allah in our actions and deeds in the effort that he judges us favourably.

The Heart is where you get to define your overall purposes in life: it contains both your religious and your material reasons for being.

We have multiple roles on this Earth. Therefore we have several purposes. Some are set for us as Muslims. Others, we have to find and devise for ourselves. To clarify your purposes, you might like to consider these questions:

a) How would you best please **Allah**?
b) How would you be of use to the **other people** who matter to you, being as excellent as you can in your role towards them?
c) How would you go about achieving good things for **yourself**?

In our time on Earth, the most important things in the world are simple: you, your family, your duty to Allah, and if you have extra ability and capacity, your duty to humanity at large.

For any humble, straightforward person, your main purposes should and must include the considerations of what role you have towards those whom you love, and who love you.

Your purpose with your family and loved ones

Remember this purpose. Even if you are disillusioned about other things, you still have a role in your family, and setting out to do it as best you can is a wonderful thing to do. What could be a greater purpose than leaving a positive impact on the people who matter to you?

For your family and loved ones, you have a role which you must attend to. This is part of your purpose on Earth.

We have multiple roles, each of which requires us to do our best at it: Child, brother, sister, father, mother, aunt, leader, provider, cook, guardian, mentor, and so on. Guidance about the role comes from common sense, and from seeking to learn about how to do a good job of it by observing others we respect, and reflecting on how best to do the role. Essentially, much of our role in family is done successfully from remembering one thing: **we are best served by putting others' needs ahead of ours.**

Empathy is the ability to understand how another people is feeling. Our Nafs is connected to other people when we make efforts to read their expressions, their emotions, all with the purpose of understanding how they are feeling and responding appropriately. Women are better at doing this than men, overall: the female Nafs is particularly attuned to reading social signals.

If we have empathy, we can behave compassionately.

Compassion is very important: it is the practise of understanding what people need, and doing something to help them to achieve what they want, or to feel better. We need compassion in our relationships with our loved ones because this is what lets us put their needs before ours: the greatest gift in a relationship.

Sometimes, when we notice that the loved one is in distress, we use our Nafs to connect to them: we feel what they are feeling. This helps us to connect to them, and offer consolation and comfort. Other times, someone who depends on us will need our help to achieve something, be it some great goal (like going to school) or something simple, like feeding or tying their shoelaces: our purpose is therefore to be there for them and help them to do the things they wish to do.

Your life has meaning when you set out to do things for the people who matter to you, and those to whom you matter. If everyone did this, then we would all be more content and fulfilled.

Your Personal goals

Your goals as a person include the things that you want to achieve for yourself: be they achievements at home or at work, or socially, or for your personal health and wellbeing. Your purposes can expand to a higher plane: many people decide that their purpose is to be of benefit to a certain section of society, or to a given field of study, so they pursue goals that help them serve this purpose.

For those of us who have not yet found a role outside of the family, you may not find out exactly what you want to do straight away, but this needs not be too much a concern: as long as you attend to your religion and your rules of Conduct, Allah will present opportunities and openings for you sooner or later.

To find an occupation that you love, keep an eye on the things that you a) enjoy doing, and b) are good at, and c) are of use to the world in some way. This is achieved by being open to new experiences, and trying many different things. Alhamdulillah, school and education gives some of us a chance to discover such things, but this is not universal: many of us do not find our strengths until later on. We are well advised to do things outside school, and alongside our jobs, pursuing our interests and meeting like-minded people, in the effort to find our niche. Be patient, and content, knowing things are exactly as they are meant to be.

So in summary, we have multiple purposes as human beings, because we have different roles. Keeping those purposes in mind will help steer us through the inevitable difficulties and hiccups along the way. When we fail at a goal, for example if we upset a loved one because we forgot to do something for them, or said something that was insensitive, we must understand that failure is never wasted: it is merely part of our education, and we can go on and correct it with optimism and courage because we keep the higher purpose in mind: we want to do a good job in our role, for the sake of Allah, and for the happiness and contentment of the people who matter.

The point of a higher purpose is to give us a sense of energising our mission, and fuelling our endurance. Life is difficult: this is guaranteed. If we keep to our mission, then we accept that there will be problems but we are able to keep our cool because we know that overall we are heading in a clear direction. There are many little missions in life, but having a strong sense of purpose helps us to pick and persist with them in a productive way.

Goals: What features does a good goal have?

So, once we have a purpose in any given context, we can now set a goal or set of goals for that context. We ask ourselves what goals we want, and create goals in an intelligent way.

Goals are best if they are somewhat ambitious. They should be bold, and require you to put in effort, but not be impossible. In other words, they stretch you in a positive way while you reach for them. A good goal obeys the following rules, best remembered by the acronym SMART.

Specific:	It should be clear what you are trying to achieve. You know when you have done it.
Measurable:	You must be able to map out how to get to it, and judge your progress towards it.
Ambitious:	It must be in tune with your reasons for living- your purpose, resident in your Heart.
Realistic:	It must be difficult but not impossible.
Timely:	It must be within a timeframe that you have set out, and try to keep.

Look at this graph, called the Yerkes Dodson Curve.

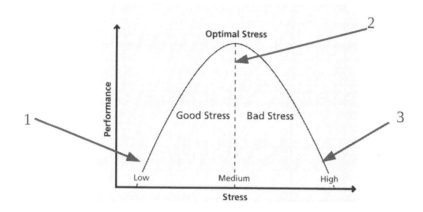

In defining a goal, you need something that will keep you on your toes- something that will cause you a degree of *productive stress*. Now stress is neither good nor bad on its own: it depends purely on the amount of it.

With no stress whatsoever (point 1), you don't have any drive- you are disinterested. With too much stress (point 3), you are overwhelmed and paralysed. So you need to find a goal that offers you a degree of difficulty that you can cope with, that brings your ability to the front- point 2. This 'sweet spot' is something that you will learn about yourself as you grow; you will gain knowledge of it more quickly if you practise reflection and self awareness with the help of Allah, and Du'aa. Everybody has a different sweet spot, depending on their own ability and their own particular goals.

Goals: How are we going to achieve them?

This is where your Intellect, being the source of planning and logic, comes into its own.

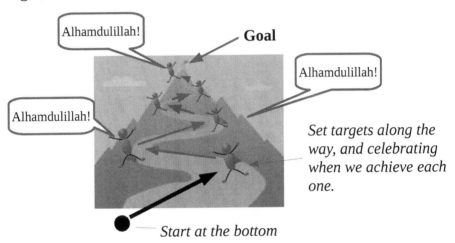

Set targets along the way, and celebrating when we achieve each one.

Start at the bottom

All goals are achieved one second at a time, one tiny step at a time. Don't stare at the mountain top: aim for next ledge only.

Your intellect is your best ally in setting out how you get to the next ledge. The secret is simple: micro-targets.

If you realise this, you will be able to break any task down to little targets and then commit yourself to work towards each. For each target, your use your intellect to estimate the time and resources you need to get them done. Be kind to yourself! Help plan your success by making the steps more visibly achievable. Define and set out what you would need to get to each little step.

It is also important to **celebrate small successes** in achieving each micro-target: it re-energises your Nafs, keeping your emotions jolly and motivated to continue towards the task from one day to the next. Taking a break to **reflect** on your success also helps you and allows you to orientate yourself towards your higher purposes or to amend your goal if you feel that you need to do so: life has a way of changing the goalposts, and we often need to adapt.

<u>Example 1: Losing weight.</u>

Take the example of someone who wants to lose weight. They chose this goal because they want to be healthy, and because they are unhappy with their appearance. They want to feel more attractive and loved. They decide to go to the gym 4 days a week, and to avoid sugary and fatty foods.

The first month goes well, going to the gym and cutting out fatty and sugary foods, but somehow the effort diminishes. They find themselves avoiding the gym, perhaps because one day the car broke down and they lost momentum, or because they don't see the weight falling off as quickly as they hoped. They start snacking on sweets because there's a bowl of sweets at their workplace.

What went wrong?
1. Unclear purpose. It was fine to want to be healthier, but the other two aims- to be more loved, and to look better- are not helpful.

The person should know that they are worthy and loved by Allah regardless, and that it is futile to influence how much others love you- this is something that we do not control. Those who truly love them would not be withholding their love for the sake of some bodyweight. 'Looking better' is subjective as well. It needs to be far more specific to be a realistic goal.

2. Lack of realism. Going to the gym 4 times a week after not going at all, is particularly tiring and dramatic. You lose energy and drive quickly; your Nafs becomes very unhappy.

3. Lack of clarity. They did not define how much weight they wanted to lose, and neither did they research how much was realistic or possible. Had they done so, they would have been far more successful at losing weight slowly and incrementally.

4. Not taking it step by step. It is important to always manage the Nafs. Expect it to be unhappy, insecure, unpredictable and uncomfortable- this is its job! Manage that by creating opportunities to focus on success and victory, for example by setting target weights each week, or by undertaking the whole weight loss plan with someone else: the Nafs loves celebrating small victories, and it is also more likely to comply with our plans when we are accountable to other people.

Example 2: Building a house

Our desire to achieve anything at all, and our eventual efforts to work towards that something, are all informed by the Nafs, Intellect and Heart. Supposing we want to build a house.

The Nafs is the most basic of drivers, and from it we have that raw energy that drives us to win, to compete, to gain status and respect, or to achieve something that accords us security and wealth. The Nafs is what drives us to have a nice, luxurious house, and it is what give us that get up and go when we are struggling with difficulties, or to face aggression and unfairness with frustration and anger. Anger is an antidote to pain: we are entitles to feel it, and we must accept it, but we are well advised not to act until we are calm. The Nafs is also behind our impulses to achieve things very quickly: to get something good, we would act on the Nafs' desire to just steal it or cheat our way to it, for example.

The Nafs, untamed, gets excessive and greedy. It would have us desire unnecessary luxury.

The Nafs is poor at planning, and wants things straight away: uncontrolled, it would have us steal the house, or to spend excessively on a house we couldn't really afford, were we to listen only to the Nafs.

We can say that whilst the Nafs' intentions may be often good, being as they come from a sense of wanting to survive and be secure, they can often get a bit out of control. So, whilst the Nafs' desires are useful, we cannot rely on them to define our goal completely, nor can we rely on the Nafs' methods: they would lead us down a troublesome path. The Nafs is useful in deciding who not to work with, because it gives us a sense of being on our guard: the Nafs is what tells us to be on alert if a person seems untrustworthy. It gives us that uneasiness we feel in our gut when something is amiss.

The Intellect is a lot more stable, and sets out to achieve things slowly, incrementally, and by cooperating with others, and by conforming to rules, systems, and knowledge. The Intellect gives us the facts and the figures of what we have, and matches them towards what we want to achieve realistically. In essence the Intellect is great at planning and organising, and delaying gratification while we work towards the end goal. The Intellect also adjusts plans and tactics according to emerging events, opportunities and difficulties.

The Intellect is extremely useful to achieve things in the material world. Were we to set out to build a house, we would use our Intellect to perhaps learn about construction, converse with other people about enlisting their help, and consider our resources and time carefully, setting things out as best we can to steadily achieve our aim.

The Heart is where our abilities and our purposes meet. The Heart is the rightful judge on why we are building the house: we want to create a space of safety, security and comfort, because of our material goals, and our wish to please Allah by helping the people we are responsible towards.

The Heart is the judge of whether the Nafs' desires are worthy, and the Heart assigns tasks to the Intellect to plan and execute. The Heart also listens to the Nafs, for signals of frustration or danger, and listens to the Intellect to see how plans are progressing.

The Heart, therefore, keeps us on mission, on task, and alert to risks without going overboard. Thinking with the Heart allows us to conduct ourselves in a way that serves our desires in a halal way, and achieving our aims in a way that keeps us focussed on the overall meaning of what we are doing.

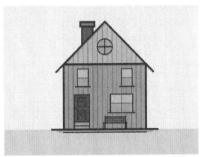

The final product sees us achieving all our dreams with great success, without an ounce of envy towards anyone else. Mission accomplished.

<u>It is all an approximation: nobody gets it perfect.</u>

Getting your goals right takes time and practice: you will often find yourself redefining them. This is perfectly OK, and in fact it is to be encouraged. Life is a series of experiments where we make the best decisions we can, at any given time, with the information we have. Plans and goals are subject to revision and change. Remember this: although people often become very focussed on finding the perfect occupation or business, this is ultimately not as important in terms of finding meaning to your life.

Your true purpose is to be good in your conduct and in your service to your God and the people who are important to you. Family, God, and humanity, are more important than work or profession, though you must also strive to become good at your individual strengths. Every goal you have must keep this in mind.

So, your purpose in life is at the root of it, merely to exist and be as good a person as you can. Your existence by itself makes you valuable and worthy to Allah. You need never devalue yourself if you keep in mind that Allah himself, far wiser and knowing, has gifted you with life. Every single hardship and obstacle is to be greeted with a belief that you are still worthy, whether you succeed in overcoming or not.

REFLECTIONS

Many people would be happier if they ask themselves
How their deeds today connect to their purpose in life.

Feeling like giving up before you get it,
Is part and parcel of achieving many a worthy goal.

If your deadlines fly by,
Then at least enjoy the whoosh when they do so.

Don't wait for success. Carry on without it.

It is easier to dream about achievement
Than to wake up and actually do it.

Succeeding in the small steps of today
Is all we can set out to do.

Material success is very rapidly abandoned
By the happiness that came with it.

When you walk with purpose,
Your destiny is to leave brighter footprints.

Failure will enlarge your spirit
If you fall back to the remembrance of Allah.

INSTANT INSIGHTS

Chapter 17: Summing up the journey

Allah tells us that we have duties and obligations both religiously and materially. In truth, Allah makes little distinction between these things. If you have good intentions and good conduct, anything you accomplish becomes a form of ibaadah (worship). Allah has given us our faculties- mental and physical, to achieve the things that we wish to do, and it is indeed a form of worship to make use of our faculties- our *mental and physical gifts*- in a way that is worthy and fulfilling.

There are plenty of books and teachings on 'productivity', 'achievement' and 'achieving greatness' and so on. There is a problem here that is worth spelling out: these books and teachings tend to imply that you are only worthy if you achieve something great, or if you access some potential within you to its maximum. The wiser truth is that you are worthy, just as you are, even if you achieve nothing at all. Achieving your potential is a worthwhile task to set out to do, sure, but you are worthy and loved by Allah whether you achieve it or not.

Allah has decided to give us life, and treasures us for simply existing. We are the highest of His creations. As such, it is our duty to believe that we are worthy and valuable right from the outset. We do not need to judge our self worth on what we achieve, or what other people think. We must believe that we are already valuable, regardless of what we do.

Regardless of how sinful or unaccomplished we feel, we are not to judge ourselves negatively, nor other people: judgment is up to Allah. We are to approach every new day as a gift, and a chance to just get on and do good things. Provided we have that intention, alhamdulillah, we are already rewarded and loved in the eyes of Allah.

Peace in our hearts, and a sense of genuine wellbeing, comes from understanding how we think, and who we are as individuals, with all of our capacities, intentions, emotions and attributes. When we match these things to a well chosen purpose, alongside obeying Allah's laws, we cannot go wrong. We will fail at many things, but failure is not our identity: it is just an educational event.

As Muslims we are not obsessed with achieving material success beyond what we need, and we define our purposes in life to be truly in keeping with things that are worthy, that would please Allah, and that see us expending our limited time on Earth merely trying to do our best for ourselves, the ones we love, and maybe for humanity at large if we are blessed with opportunity, vision and ability to do so.

We must expect, and look forward to, making mistakes. There is no such thing as failure- it is only feedback. It helps us to get closer to success. As long as we are *turning up to life*, and mindful of what we learn, we are getting closer to success both on our own behalf and in the path of Allah.

Islam has within its very meaning a message of peace through submission: We need to make peace with the things we cannot change. Some of our deeds will cause us so much shame that we cannot dare to talk to anyone about them: that is fine, as long as we talk to Allah about them, seeking His forgiveness and resolving to not repeat them. Sometimes we will learn from our mistakes, other times we will not. We must accept our limitations: there are some faults of ours which will be beyond repair or correction. Our task, then, would be to avoid the circumstances where those faults would show up, while working towards an environment where our strengths are at their best.

All of this stakes time, and effort, and humility. We just need to put in the effort, and keep our intentions good. The results are in the hands of Allah. Alhamdulillah.

REFLECTIONS

INSTANT INSIGHTS

Printed in Great Britain
by Amazon